A Country Planet

A Country Planet

Woodlots, Pig Plows, Tax Shelters, and 20 More Fresh Approaches to Rural Success

Tim Matson
Photographs by the author

THE COUNTRYMAN PRESS
Woodstock, Vermont

Thanks to Dominique Mintz for the author's photograph on page 82.

Library of Congress Cataloging-in-Publication data

Matson, Tim, 1943–
Country planet.

1. Country life—Vermont—Orange County—Addresses, essays, lectures. 2. Orange County (Vt.)—Social life and customs—Addresses, essays, lectures.
3. Matson, Tim, 1943– —Addresses, essays, lectures.
I. Title.
S521.V5M38 1986 974.3′63 85–17440
ISBN 0–88150–052–6 (pbk.)

Some of these stories first appeared, in slightly different form, in *Country Journal, Fine Homebuilding, Mother Earth News, Harrowsmith, Farmstead, The Valley News, Small Farmer's Journal, New England Farm Bulletin, The New England Gardener, Acres,* U.S.A. and *Yankee.*

Designed and produced by Robinson Book Associates

Printed in the United States by Capital City Press

CONTENTS

WATER

ACKNOWLEDGMENTS

It would take another book to say thanks to everyone who helped, so I'll simply put in a good word for editors, often unrecognized, who encouraged me along the way: Lynn Ascrizzi, John Barstow, Jake Chapline, Tim Clark, Steve Gordon, Roger Holmes, Bob Kaldenbach, Carrie Kent, James Lawrence, Lynn Miller, and Charles Walters, Jr.

Thanks also to Bob Gere, of Sun Photo, for his silvery darkroom work.

To David Robinson, for his design work.

To my publisher, Peter Jennison, who makes it all come together.

And most of all, to Ellen Langtree, partner, critic, and inspiration.

Other Books by Tim Matson

Pilobolus
Earth Ponds
Alternative Light Styles

PREFACE

On a sun-baked August afternoon fifteen years ago I began a short vacation in Vermont. It was my first trip to the Northeast Kingdom and I camped in a hayloft on a farm outside Lyndonville. I remember mudcaked hogs and hard cider and midnights so sharp I thought I was walking on the stars. Back in the city, I couldn't get the mountains out of my dreams. A year later I quit my job and moved to Orange County.

In exchange for an editor's desk, I bought a wood stove, a chainsaw, and a pair of felt-lined Sorels. The old farmhouse I rented was frigid and the chainsaw died. But the roughest part was finding work. Eventually I bluffed my way onto a construction crew building barns for $2.50 an hour. I took home more than the minimum wage. This was the first stage of my apprenticeship in rural affairs, and it led to an experimental schooling in the basic country elements: shelter, homegrown food, water, and the woods. I was working 300 miles north of New York City, but it seemed I'd moved to another planet.

This book is a collection of the articles and essays that grew out of my experiences. It is, essentially, a report from a backyard think tank and proving ground. If it adds any to the sweetness and survival of rural life I'll be satisfied.

T. M.
Strafford, Vermont
August, 1985

IN THE BEGINNING

It was a season of few words. I found a mountain woodlot thick with evergreens and hardwoods. I cleared a campsite, unrolled my sleeping bag, and set up the old Kimball piano under a poplar tree. That camp was home for three months while I built my house.

$50.00 tent.

That's the first mention of the tent in my log book. It must have been July 1st because that's the day I drove down to White River Junction to pay off the lawyer for getting me the deed to the land. Then I walked around the corner to a sports outfitter and found a blue-and-white-striped canvas tent, cabana style, like a miniature A&W Root Beer stand. On the box was a color shot of a burly guy in a lawn chair beside the tent, and a perfectly put together brunette, slippery and tan, emerging from a green swimming pool. The tent was on sale. Who could resist?

July 4th! Two days of digging and it begins. Seven poles up and the shape is a sun scoop. Weather hot. Beer gone.

The page I'm looking at is white schoolbook note paper, blue lined, covered with red and green ink notes and sketches, a brown stain (creosote or coffee?), and a paragraph in type:

Second nite in tent. Slept well. Tonight full moon rising over rolling mist.

That was the first and last time I tried typing in the tent. After that the neat black print disappears.

Next, there's a sketch of the house plan, or rather the location for the poles I was using for the main uprights. That's as far as I had planned. The Xs signify the poles I'd erected, the dots were the poles to come. The shape was pretty much dictated by the land. I'd started out to build a rectangle, but a rock blocked the digging, so I added a prow pointing west, schooner cabin style.

2 x 10s arrive from Lyman's Mill, first big rig up the mountain, busted his mirror on a balsam tree.

I remember the smell of those balsams. I was surrounded by balsams, and in the heat they put out a terrific resinous bouquet. I also remember the smell of the tent. When the canvas heated up in the sun, it smelled like hemp. Canvas is made from hemp. It was a resinous summer all around.

The tent had a floor about six feet square. The walls rose at a slight inward angle to five feet or so, and then tucked in to the blue and white hip roof that was suspended at the center by exterior aluminum poles. There was a double door—choice of canvas or a breeze screen—and a small window screen with a canvas flap. Duck to step in, and you'd have found a sleeping bag on a mattress, two kerosene lights, tool box, conga drum, chainsaw, box of food, tiny gas cartridge stove, Norwegian portable radio, and, stuffed away in the driest corner, my camera and the typewriter. Tight quarters. With its aluminum skeleton on the outside and me on the inside, I sometimes felt as if I'd been swallowed by a canvas crustacean.

There's not much about the tent in the log book, and I hate to say it, but somewhere along the line the tent got left out in the rain—MacArthur Park Style—and rotted. But I kept the poles. Now I use them in the garden to stake tomatoes. The garden grows exactly where the tent was pitched, so there's a pattern there.

July 8th. Strong sensation of being the first to settle this land. Working today in the heat, anger, flies, sweat and swear, evening overcast, long evening swim in the big pond.

I'll never forget those deer flies. They could bite right through your shirt and leave a hole in the sleeve.

It was rough stripping the bark off the balsams. It had to be done right after dropping the tree or the bark would dry out and cement itself on. After a day of felling and limbing and shaving bark, I'd hike down the road to the trout pond and cool off. Later I'd walk back to the site and sit, lotus style, in front of the fire after dark to sketch out the next day's work. The house was a total improvisation. Last night's fantasies, tomorrow's foundation.

July 15. More poles going up. Thunderstorms. Took a fall.

Putting up those poles was a hair-raising event. I had cut and debarked a dozen 20-foot balsams and dug 5-foot holes in the ground. The object was to get the poles planted in the holes and then build the house around them. I'd roll a pole into position with the butt end over the hole and then lift the top. When it worked right, I could get the butt to drop right in and then walk the pole up as I came in.

But the poles were slippery and heavy, and sometimes they'd kick out and really throw me. As the poles went up, it looked as if I was putting the trees I'd cut back up, but naked, stripped. A strange sight. I'd sit by the fire after dark and watch the flames reflect off the pale wood. They stood out against the forest like totems.

The poles totally changed my orientation as a carpenter. I'd been accustomed to building everything with milled lumber, nice and square. But landing on this

45-acre woodlot switched my view from angular to circular. My note paper is jammed with sketches—log furniture, log houses, pole barns. Instead of nails, everything had to be connected with 12-inch bolts.

July 20. Saturday eve. $288 for lumber to Duncan MacIntosh in Corinth. Milky Way brighter than I've ever seen it. Big sky here! creosoted the floor joists. Next: flooring . . .

The tent was headquarters. By day I went out to battle the balsams, then I retreated to the tent at night to lick my wounds and swig some beer. Sometimes I'd listen to CBC on the Tandberg.

It would be sultry and dark. A couple of tree frogs chorusing back and forth overhead. I'm sitting outside the tent by the fire. In the tent there's a beeswax candle burning, and the blue and white stripes glow. At the edge of the clearing, I can see the poles pointing to the sky. I pull the tarp off the Kimball and start to play. When I quit, the fire's out. I'm surrounded by fireflies. My neighbors down the valley told me they knew I hadn't cracked my skull when they heard the piano echoing in the night.

July 27 . . . Big Day, sub floor on, lookin' good, deliberating roof shape. Got all the plates up. Worked out simple plan to put on roof boards and then frame it from inside.

That summer I shot just two black-and-white pictures of the tent. One accidentally, at the beginning of the roll, as I was winding the film onto the spool. I'm standing in front of the tent, maybe ten feet away. The tent is tilting down into the left hand corner of the frame like a sinking ship. Just off to the right, there's a thick pine slab up on sap buckets: my kitchen counter and work bench. It's a handsome pine slab, two inches thick and six feet long. I still have it. It resembles a trout with a knot for an eye. On the bench, left to right, there's the Tandberg radio, playing bluegrass, I'd wager. There's an enamel cup, no doubt full of coffee. Empty beer bottle. Chainsaw. Clipping shears. A roll of toilet paper. All the essentials. And looming up just behind the tent, a cluster of poles and 2 x 10s, the framework of the house. Cross-checking with the log book, I'd say the photo must have been taken at the end of July.

The other shot of the tent was taken a few days later. It's a moody composition, chunks of shadow and light. The view right into the tent. Judging by the shadows, the time is late afternoon. The open tent door cuts a bright patch in the black shadow on the back wall. It's the shape of a house with a steep pitched roof. Below, on the sleeping bag, there's a newspaper lying flat in the slanting sun, illuminated just enough so if you look real close you can see the headline: NIXON RESIGNS AT NOON TODAY. There's no mention of that day in the log book. Just the picture, carefully composed. That one look in the tent. History.

September 29. Living in the kitchen with a woodstove. Double floor up front just begun. Home and hoping for good vibes.

SHELTER

ZOOT

This is the Zoot. It's a blend of greenhouse, bay window, and louver. For good luck there's something old—the low-relief wood brace, and something new—thermal pane. The Zoot faces south. That's the reason it's a 3-D triangle. It's a great way to get a south window on a wall that faces west. The triangle creates illusions. From outside, due south, you see one big horizontal mass. From the west, vertical glass. From dead ahead it's just the Zoot.

The southern glass is fixed, but the west window can open like a wind scoop. It pulls in the mountain breeze and ventilates the house and plants. In spring, flowers and vegetables are born in the Zoot. I planned the greenhouse and the scoop, but the light came as a surprise. You see, it's right next to the front door, so a kerosene lamp in the Zoot turns into a porch light at night, and that's a welcome sight.

Putting the finishing touches on a Vermont tax shelter. Roll roofing rates Below Average on Form 491, so the builder decided to bring it all the way to the ground, beating the west wind and the high taxes on roofing and siding.

TAX SHELTERS

Sure as mud roads and red-winged blackbirds signal spring in the Green Mountains of Vermont, so, too, vernal flocks of tax listers arrive flapping their papers, clacking yardsticks, and poking into their neighbors' nests. Tipped off by building permits, they home in on dwellings and barns, new and remodeled alike. Once permitted to enter a house, they hiss and claw over windows and kitchen counters, light fixtures and floors. They especially like to turn up the carpet to see what may have been swept under the rug; they prefer to find hardwoods. Since the tax lister is a protected species, and it's a crime to shoot one out of season, the afflicted house is certain to suffer some damage, most often in the form of a painfully sharp bill stuck in the mailbox.

What can be done to guard against the ravages of the tax lister? While many country heads have hardened up after a decade of grinding out double-digit R-factors, only a few have learned how to shelter their homes against tax loss. For some, the following precautions will come too late. Once appraised, always appraised—allowances for depreciation and discounts at grievance meetings notwithstanding. But if your dream house has not yet become an annual nightmare on the town-report delinquent list, take heed.

Let's start with a lister's eye view. Most dwellings in Vermont are seen in the light of Form 491, published by James Knowles, Jr. and Associates, Appraisers, Northeast Harbor, Maine. Similar charts affect homes all across the country. Reverently referred to as "The Card" by my hometown listers, 491 is an ominous yellow 8 x 10 index of all household trappings deemed taxable. From foundation to roof, more than 30 components are vulnerable, and each is awarded an appraisal ranging from Below Average to Average to Good to Excellent. The higher the rating, the more it hurts.

For instance, a poured concrete foundation is Excellent, followed in descending order by block, pier and post. Exterior walls covered with clapboards or wood shingles rate Excellent; aluminum siding is Average; boards or plywood Below Average. (Still wonder why those back road folk never get around to finished siding?) Cedar shingles top the list of roofing, followed by metal, asphalt shingles, roll roofing, and last and surely least, tar paper. As yet no rating has been attached to sod. However, there is a rating for design, and complexity is deemed Excellent. One lister warned, "Just build a straight house. It's cheaper."

To make the system accountable, ratings are scaled on a point system: Excellent gets a 10, Good 8, Average 6, Below Average 4. What if you mix your materials? Perhaps your foundation is a mix of concrete posts and cinder block, like one of my neighbors'. Or perhaps the walls are a mosaic of board and plaster and drywall. Blending materials seems to lower the overall rating. There is no room in the formula for part Excellent and part Below Average. One former town lister keeps the back wall of his house sheathed in rough boards while putting a respectable clapboard face forward. It's the best of both worlds at excursion rates. As veteran lister Mrs. K told me, "The tax business is very subjective. Sometimes I just don't see things." Her husband was more succinct: "It's a complicated mess."

A few items, though, are straightforward. Rooms, bedrooms, and bathrooms are toted up, along with square footage. The higher the sum, the higher the tax. Valuations are tacked to several features: an oil furnace is tagged between $2,000 and $3,000; a wood furnace at $4,000; and a woodstove won't cost you a dime. Electrical hookups are worth $150 for 200 amp, $120 for 100 amp; a fireplace is valued at $750; and underground plumbing at $350. Out of all these points—rooms, footage, and dollars—comes the structure's Estimated Reproduction Cost. The appraisal is then multiplied by 1% and taxed at the town rate. For example, in my town the tax rate is $5.34. For a house valued at $50,000, that means 50 multiplied by $5.34, or a tax of $267. (These figures don't include land tax—that's another story.)

Naturally, the home builder who calculates the solar energy falling on his site, but neglects to look at The Card, invites the lister to black out his savings. "I always tell people who are building to go to the town clerk's office and look at The Card," Mrs. K told me. "But not many do."

Marty M. is one of my neighbors who wishes he had looked at his card before remodeling the house he bought ten years ago. His dishwasher, installed under the kitchen counter, is considered taxable. "The dishwasher is assessed at $388," Marty told me, "so it runs us $20 a year in taxes. That's $200 since we installed it. On wheels in the same place, no tax." Marty winced. He pointed to another financial drain in the kitchen. "They tax these cabinets I built in. If I had built hutches instead, they couldn't touch us. It's just a matter of four nails, but it costs hundreds. You have to make a lot of aesthetic compromises to get ahead."

Dave and Elaine V. built their first house not long ago, and they knew about The Card. They grew up in town with a couple of listers for kin. So they designed the place with one eye on the blueprints and the other on tax shelters. Instead of building a basement, they poured concrete pillars for a foundation. They nailed up random-width rough boards for interior and exterior walls. To cover the floor they laid one-inch plywood, tax-exempt because it rates as subflooring already counted in the footage. For a chimney they chose removable insulated metal stovepipe rather than masonry; on that component they save about $50 a year. Their house tax is $300 a year; comparable new "finished" dwellings are taxed two or three times higher.

Nothing is wrong or right about taxes. After all, folks must support their schools and roads. But with town budgets sky high, builders should be aware that it's the new house that pays the inflated tax. "People building nowadays get hit hardest," Mrs. K admitted. She feels pressure each year to come up with the extra money needed to meet the budget. "People complain that the listers make your taxes," she said. "But it's the people at the town meeting voting every spring to raise the budget."

Perhaps it's mountain justice: invading flatlanders who raise their hands to vote for cafe-society services should foot the bill. On the other hand, there's nothing stopping newcomers and natives alike from taking a close look at their cards before making any bets on a house.

MUDROOMS

Lately I've become a connoisseur of mudrooms. I've been scanning the countryside for specimens of mudroom design, taking shots, and bringing them home to add to my mudroom bestiary, a collection of photographs I plan to consult as soon as I build a mudroom of my own. I say bestiary because the mudroom embodies a unique architectural species. Rarely will you find two alike. Some are plain homemade, some ornamental. Often they say something about the people behind the door.

At its simplest, the mudroom is an enclosed entry way, usually annexed, where you can stomp the dirt or snow off your boots, or remove them, and hang up coat and hat, before entering. More sophisticated mudrooms combine the advantages of the shakedown entry way with an airlock for conserving heat. Other facets of mudroom design can produce payoffs in refrigeration, storage space, shelter for critters, solar power, and so forth.

The mudroom appears to have humble farmhouse origins, coinciding with the elimination of earthen floors. In Japan, where it's customary to slip off your shoes before entering a dwelling, the mudroom is known as the *genken*; it's been a cornerstone of Japanese architecture since the twelfth century. In Vermont, the mudroom has been a popular architectural tradition since the first settlers kicked off their boots. It has sheltered the thresholds of taverns, inns, schoolhouses, stores, farmhouses, and homes. The newest mudroom in my neighborhood is a portable entry to the general store. It's a three-piece modular unit—roof, walls, door—that is assembled in November and taken away in May.

"It's great," the storekeeper told me. "Keeps out the snow and keeps in the heat. The girls at the cash registers were freezing. They love it."

Apart from the rare roving mudroom, most domestic varieties set up house for keeps, and one of the best places to learn about the standard breed mudroom is in a one-room schoolhouse. There can't have been many places more in need of it. Kids have the knack of tracking in more debris per square inch than the rest of humankind put together. Send a dozen or more through the same door five days a week, nine months a year, and the advantages of the mudroom become clear. In one nearby village, I came upon a century-old crimson

schoolhouse recently converted into a community center, complete with solar greenhouse on the south wall. Jutting out from the same wall stands the mudroom, which the designer wisely left intact. The mudroom is roughly 10 feet by 10 feet and capped with a hip roof. The floor is a thick concrete slab, perhaps the best defense against the march of the Vermont seasons. There are benches for unlacing boots, pegs to hang wet clothes, and a couple of large windows to provide natural light.

Another good lesson lies in the schoolhouse elevation, two steps above mudroom level. In winter, when the mudroom door is opened to the schoolroom, heat resists spilling out. This is an airlock conservation measure pioneered by Neanderthal-era Eskimos. They built tunnelways into their igloos a foot or two below the dwelling level.

Indeed, there's a lot to be learned in a schoolhouse mudroom, pitfalls included. In this instance, the hip roof. Apart from a prejudice I have against this umbrella design, as a mudroom entry way roof, it flunks. The watershed pattern drenches all eaves. Gutters are one solution, I suppose, but I'm accustomed to seeing roof ice twist them around like Budweiser pop tops. I'd choose instead a peaked roof with the gable over the mudroom door.

At the opposite end of the spectrum you'll find the micro mudroom. It tends to be a homemade add-on, often not much bigger than a telephone booth. (Any day now I'm expecting to find an old phone booth planted at the front of a glassy solar dwelling; what better way to recycle all those phone booths displaced by plastic hoods?) Built on a foundation of posts, stone, or concrete piers, the micro mudroom may not be as durable or spacious as the one sitting on a concrete slab, but then it's more manageable to finance and construct. After all, it *is* just a mudroom. Stud-wall wood-frame construction is the norm, as is the lack of insulation, unless the mudroom is to be heated, or treated like a hermetically sealed airlock. And I'd look for at least one window in the door or the wall. Nobody needs a gloomy mudroom—mud season's dreary enough already.

One architect I know likes to station a mudroom on each of his buildings. It adds a beguiling touch to the structure and a personal stamp to his work. You can't mistake his hometown; its main street is flanked with three-dimensional thresholds: tall and narrow, some with arched doors, some with curved roofs, some with steep gables. Most stand at homefronts, but one doubles as an airlock and clodbuster for a local tavern. Stepping through it I'm reminded of the ticket booth to the Tunbridge World's Fair. Another of his mudrooms features a domed door with a tiny leaded window, and a steep pitched roof. It looks like a sentinel hut at Buckingham Palace.

Since a mudroom may tend to look like an outhouse, I will resist the temptation to carve a quarter moon in the window shutters. One embellishment I will add is the grate dirt remover. This is a salvaged heat register set into the floor in place of a door mat, preferably vintage cast iron to rebuff kicking, mudcaked feet. The register collects dirt and snow which drops into an inset cleanout box, or clear through the floor if you don't mind the draft.

The bigger the mudroom, the better the storage. It's a good place to keep a cat or hang a side of beef (not simultaneously). Some people install an unplugged refrigerator or an insulated storage box to preserve food, fuel free, in winter. There's only one thing crazier than a hip roof, and that's running the fridge during a Vermont winter. Mudrooms intended for cold storage work best on the shadowy north side of the house. Over on the sunny side, a mudroom equipped with coldframe glazing can grow vegetables and flowers. Now there's a designer's dilemma with just one solution: the two-mudroom house.

STOVES I HAVE KNOWN

If ever there was a fitting subject for the school of hard knocks, it's the wood stove. I learned about wood stoves at home tending close to a dozen different space heaters and furnaces. There is more yet to learn, but that means more winters and extra home study. Wood burning isn't taught; it's experienced. You won't even find it practiced in public, except perhaps around a pot of beans on the chunk stove at town meeting.

I remember my first stove the way some people remember their first automobile: a ticket to independence. It was an Ashley Automatic. A couple of decades ago everybody with a wood pile in the yard kept an Ashley in the house. The Ashley (which is still in production) stands on four cast iron legs. The fire burns in a black, oval, sheet-metal firebox that sports dual cast iron loading doors, one on the front, the other a hatch on top. It's a parlor stove built in several sizes which are of varying capacity, but the overall design is consistent. The top hatch permits loading to the very top of the stove, above the level of the front door. This hatch also allows the option of burning logs vertically. With its black metal vault and shiny chrome front door handle, my old Ashley might have been a bank safe. And it was, when you count the money saved by burning wood.

It was an easy stove to fire because it lacked an interior baffle. Thus the Ashley wasn't particularly efficient, which is not to say it wasn't hot. The light, thin steel firebox heated up rapidly and the stove radiated plenty of heat. In fact, a good hot fire prompted the black firebox cheeks to blush red.

The front door damper gave the Ashley its character. Mounted on the square iron door was a small steel box with a chrome dial. A turn of the dial regulated a damper inside the box, controlling the flow of air through the door vent down to the base of the fire. But this wasn't any run-of-the-mill damper. This was automatic. You'd light the fire, set the dial, and surrender control to the thermostat. The prospect of starting a stove wide open and walking out on it was as revolutionary as driving without a gear shift. Old stoves, unattended, were guaranteed to overheat and die after an intense burn, if they didn't spark a fire and burn the house down first.

A bimetal spring controlled the Ashley. When the stove burned low, during ignition for instance, the spring opened the damper to swig fresh air for the accelerating fire. But as the stove heated to operating temperature, the spring closed the damper to a pre-selected narrow airflow. The stove was set on course for a long warm voyage. As the engineers explain it, this is metal "with a memory." The steel spring expanded and contracted according to the heat.

But an automatic shift isn't foolproof. The Ashley was purring warmly one January afternoon when a cardboard box full of day-old baby chickens arrived at the house. I set the box beside the Ashley to keep them warm. That night I adjusted the damper for a low fire and went to bed. I woke up in the middle of a midnight gale. Smoke was billowing up the stairs. I rushed down and found the red hot Ashley lighting up the darkened living room, and a box of fried chicken. The cardboard blazed. I heaved the burning box out the door. The ashes sizzled in the snow. No wonder they named it the Ashley. Then I heard the wind, gusting hard from the north, so hard that, despite the low setting on the stove's valve, the Ashley had overheated and ignited the box. That night I learned my first important lesson in stove keeping: Do Not Order Baby Chicks in January. There is a corollary to go with that: Respect Your Stove Clearances. To those lessons I added the option to override the automatic damper by installing a manual stovepipe damper just above the exhaust vent. The effect was to throw the Ashley into reverse, recreating a nineteenth-century parlor stove, minus the nice designs.

Fortunately there was a wood furnace in the cellar. "Wise, Akron, Ohio," read the stamp on the loading door, confirming an owlish appearance to the thing, perfected with one blinking fiery eye. The furnace consisted of a barrel-sized iron firebox encased in a circular sheet metal plenum. The plenum held an envelope of hot air around the furnace. Six tubular heat ducts spoked out from the top of the plenum, connected to heat registers in the living room floor. These ducts delivered the heat up into the house by natural convection. A loop of hot air turned whenever the furnace burned.

This is the way the pros heat, said the farmer who rented me the house. Indeed, the owl took advantage of the two natural forces that hill people traditionally worship: gravity and lift. Down went the firewood through a window into the cellar, up wafted the heat into the house. It wasn't necessary to tramp down cellar very often because a control chain linked the furnace damper to the living room.

As fitted to the house, the system had one obvious flaw. The furnace exhausted through an exterior brick chimney on the south wall. A mammoth mass of passive heat was wasted to the outdoors and the chimney clogged with creosote like an old artery. Our chimney fires lit up the mountains.

But inside that house was a fullness of heat I've never quite matched since. It was enhanced by a generous humidity level sustained by the steaming two-gallon water reservoir built into the furnace wall. In truth, this was more than a wood furnace—it was an indoor weather system. The air stayed in motion even in summer, when cool air welling up from the cellar was a blessing. Too cool was not a problem, nor too hot, because the registers could be closed off.

In spite of the control chain, I found myself gravitating down the cellar stairs. I'd sit on the splitting stump face to face with the owl and watch its eye flicker and blink. The iron creaked. Sparks popped. It was a place of glory in the surrounding harvest of firewood and canned vegetables. Too bad it was so isolated down there. I liked the companionship of the fire, but I didn't take to the loneliness of the long distance stove keeper. It helped that there was a barrel of cider under the stairs.

Eventually, I left the house. I coached the new tenant in the art of setting underground fires, and I told him that this was the way the pros keep warm. He switched to oil, I heard.

The next wood stove was a nineteenth-century cast iron cooking range set up in the kitchen of the house I was building. "Standard G" read the Gothic letters on the black oven door. Chrome trim edged the cooking surface, over a wide-hipped oven and firebox. It stood on shapely legs. The gender was visibly feminine.

I connected the range to a stovepipe that zigzagged up and out an opening in the wall and clamped to the eave of the roof. The stove smoked. No matter how much I tightened up the old firebox, no matter how often I cleaned the pipe, it smoked. Bring back the draft! Later I installed an insulated steel chimney straight through the roof. The Standard G blazed. Truly, the path to enlightenment is straight up.

Oil shortages in the mid-Seventies triggered a stampede to buy wood stoves. Pretty soon there was also a shortage of stoves. Compound that with the appearance of ancient woodburners and you can picture the Seventies' gallop to wood—it ran backwards. Backwards to nineteenth-century chunk stoves, cooking ranges and furnaces. Why so? Aside from Ashleys and a few imported Scandinavians with microscopic fireboxes, there wasn't much else. It seemed the whole countryside had chucked modern technology, lit up the old burners, and joined the Luddites.

The mood was catchy. I wanted another stove. But I didn't look forward to repeating the mistakes of outdated stove builders. For awhile I lived in a village house heated by a new Riteway stove. It was more like a living room furnace, complete with large rectangular firebox and a bimetal automatic damper. A nervous few months. It was impossible to damp down the stove without caking the chimney and stove with creosote.

Had I been handy with an acetylene torch, I might have built my own stove. That was how the real pros did it. One neighbor had welded together a customized steel stove for his house. It consisted of massive slabs of diamond plate steel holding the fire beneath a cooking surface big as a billiard table; perfect for a big house on a mountaintop full of gourmet cooks. That's where I discovered that the best food on earth comes from the oven of a wood stove.

I soon met another designer working on a custom burner. We had been teamed up by a contractor to build a vacation house for a family of flatlanders. Eric Darnell was his name and he called his stove the Free Flow. After a day pounding nails, he'd drive home and weld on the stove. One winter evening after work I stopped by at Eric's place. It was a tiny old chicken coop he'd converted into a home, with a shed roof tilting north and a wide-angle bay window facing south. Toward the back of the room stood a weird arrangement of curved steel pipes—the Free Flow. I could see that it was a stove because out of one end emerged a stovepipe connected to the chimney. Otherwise, it looked like a pipe fitter's nightmare.

"Boomerangs," Eric said, "think of crossed boomerangs." He told me that he'd been inspired by the aerodynamics of some boomerangs he had designed and carved. Sure, I nodded with a shiver. I noticed the cat food was frozen in its dish. Eric lit the fire and I felt the stove come to life. Eleven curved steel truck exhaust pipes started sucking cool air up off the floor and pumping it out above the fire chamber, hot. In minutes the room zoomed from 30°F to 75°F. A warm breeze fanned the place. The cat got interested in its food.

"It's a suction blower," Eric explained. He pulled off his wool hat and shook down a foot-long pony tail. "Absolutely silent, no electric fan. The air comes up from the floor and through the tubes and is expanded by the heat and blown into the room."

Eric had started with the parlor stove concept, integrated a Scandinavian-style interior baffle, and then added an ingenious flair: a burning chamber formed of pipes that cradled the fire and pumped hot air.

"The Free Flow uses naturally induced convection currents," he added, "so you're getting force as well as heat. The Free Flow gives you tremendous circulation plus twice the surface area because of the tubes. They are mostly buried within the stove. You gain on heat transfer with much less going up the chimney. Air passes through the stove three times."

I was amazed. And warm. I wanted one. But this was the prototype, and it would be a year before Eric put together a squad of stove builders and started the Free Flow Stove Works on the site of an abandoned copper mine in Strafford. Eventually I took home Number 176.

Since then, I've spent nine warm winters with the Free Flow. It's like living with a woodburning windmill. The Free Flow will warm up a cold house faster than any stove I know. Best of all, it combines the natural air circulation of the old cellar furnace with the companionship of a parlor stove. And because it uses tubes to wick away the warmth, the stove never overheats. That means longevity for the stove, and for the stove keeper, the ultimate reward: a good night's sleep, uninterrupted.

CABIN CELLAR

If I had to get back to the land again, I'd go by cabin cellar. Getting there may be half the fun, but not if you're swamped the first summer with a marathon of chores on top of house building: clearing brush, chopping wood, fighting off black flies and zoning officers. Too often the house winds up uncomfortably rough and out of plumb.

After hurriedly pouring a $10,000 six-sided concrete foundation, a friend of mine went into the red and stayed there for two years before finishing his elaborate place. One newcomer fresh from a decade of teaching Plato in New Jersey set out to lay his first concrete-block foundation. By October he was still at it and had to hire two men to help build his family an emergency cabin. Now I know why native builders start out living in the basement, with the first floor for a roof. Or in a trailer. A cabin cellar makes even better sense. It's as snug as living on a yacht.

For the novice builder, a cabin cellar is a proving ground. The structure is small and simple, offering practice in all aspects of building, from siting to roofing. And if you slip up it's no big deal to go backwards and fix your mistake. "It's playschool carpentry," an architect I know said approvingly. On the other hand, if you're skilled, the structure goes up fast. That leaves time and energy for other chores, like growing a garden to fill the cellar.

My cabin cellar evolved according to the great American principle of afterthought. I began with a simple plan for a root cellar. I sidetracked a friend on his bulldozer, and he carved a seven-foot deep pit in the slope 30 paces north of home. The cellar hole was a clean six-feet wide, the length of his blade. The slope was well contoured for drainage, and the soil came up sandy and dry. A perfect site for a root cellar.

From the woods I milled a thousand feet of rot-resistant hemlock planks to build the cellar. But when it came time for framing, I reconsidered. My house, chicken coop, and woodshed all stood on wood pilings. Time for a change. I choose cement block and hired Homer Kingsbury to help. By hand we mixed and poured a six-foot by nine-foot footing around an earth floor, and the blocks piled up. Again the vision grew. Better than a sod roof on top, I imagined a cabin workshop. Covering the foundation with dirt would be just throwing it away.

And I already had the lumber. This time I asked Ellen, my new spouse, to help raise the block walls another course to seven feet, just above ground level on the high side of the hill.

A visitor looked suspicious when I showed him the new root cellar. "Don't kid me," he said. "You're getting ready for the big one to drop." After that, I began to see even more potential for the cabin cellar.

Next I assembled an eight-inch-thick, double-boarded platform 10 feet by 10 feet, cantilevered over the cellar and insulated with fiberglass batts. I put a hatch in the middle of the floor, a ladder in the cellar, and vents through the walls to pull in cool air at ground level and exhaust warm air up top.

On the platform, I built a south facing micro-Cape peaked with a 12-foot ridge. I ordered two truckloads of topsoil to backfill the cellar walls. Then I built a spruce bin the size of a steamer trunk and lowered it into the cellar. I stocked it full of homegrown spuds and added shelves and barrels stuffed with turnips, beets, and carrots. Upstairs, I moved in my desk and typewriter.

Completed, the cabin cellar is a non-electric powerhouse. In summer, it's a

cold storage for perishables too bulky for the gas refrigerator (last year's potatoes kept through June). The cellar temperature holds between 45° and 55°F, cold enough to keep milk and cream several days, yogurt and cheese even longer. The cool climate is ideal for fermenting homemade beer and wine, and it'll put a sparkling cold sweat on a case of ale. Right now the shelves are loaded with cabbages and red raspberry wine.

In winter, the cellar helps conserve cabin heat, as well as the crops from the garden. With vents closed, the cellar temperature settles down to just above freezing. Upstairs, gable windows draw lots of light and solar heat. And it's cheap: less than $1,000, including materials and a few days' help with the blocks.

NOTES FROM THE UNDERGROUND

The old man was talking about the house where he was born and its secret. His father had built the place on top of a deep stone cellar that spanned the length and breadth of the house. Each autumn after harvest, potatoes, carrots, cabbage, and turnips were stored down there. When times got rough in the Great Depression, his father walked out into the woods and shot deer. He butchered them down in the big cellar. Some venison was kept for the family and some was sold. It was a way to get by.

"One day," he told me, "word got around that the game warden was going to pay a visit. I never saw my dad work so fast. He started hauling stone and mixing cement, and he even got his brother to help. They built a wall down there in the cellar and made a room. You wouldn't know it was there because the door was hidden behind the cellar stairwell. That's where he kept the meat. Sure enough, when the warden drove up he looked round and headed for the cellar. But he came up and just shook his head. And he never came back. You know, that cellar was so cold you could shoot a deer in July and age it perfect!"

It was my neighbor's reminiscence that set me to musing about cellars and their part in the underground economy, past and present. Indeed, the best cellars seem to snub the establishment and radiate self-reliance. I grew up in a house with a cavernous cellar, but it had long since been converted from cold storage to coal storage. It wasn't until I settled in northern New England that I became acquainted with the cellar as a sort of outlaw's Fort Knox.

During a high-spirited apprenticeship to some backwoods beer makers, I learned what a crucial ingredient a cellar could be. Down cellar were the year-round cool temperatures required for the lengthy fermentation of premium beer. In fact, the term *lager* comes from the German word for storage. And the cellar offered something else: a place to conceal contraband. Many of the brewers I met had bottled their first lagers during Prohibition, and, like poaching venison, it was a way to make the rent and fill the belly. I listened to tales about cellars with a secret recess, a false floor, and a wood pile with a hollow core. (Once, a dusty Prohibition brew was unearthed, and after a polite no thanks, reinterred.)

I told my neighbor that every house should have a secret cellar.

"It's funny, " he said. "The house I live in now has a television in the cellar. That's progress." He did not laugh.

HOMEGROWN

THE PIG IS MIGHTIER THAN THE PLOW

Every spring I go out and buy a new tractor. I get to run it around the garden from May to November. It breaks ground, raises rocks, spreads manure, and builds up the soil. Then, around Thanksgiving, we eat the tractor. Or part of it anyway. The rest we brine, smoke and freeze. We call it the pig tractor.

Pig tractors run about 35 bucks nowadays, but I remember when you could get one for about half that. That was before so many gardeners and small farmers wanted one. Used to be just farmers raising hogs in the barn. Now everybody wants the one-pig-power garden cultivator, and they fetch a fat price.

It's worth it. Around May Day you pick up a freshly weaned shoat, hocks thin as cooking spoons and bristles just beginning to thicken. Your brand new piglet can't weight much more than 25 pounds. But by Thanksgiving, well maintained and fueled, he'll dress out to ten times that, not counting scrapple. That's the astounding thing about a pig tractor. He starts out barely strong enough to hoe dandelions and finishes up plowing 50-pound stones. Who ever heard of a rototiller that gained power as it grew older?

As far as parking goes, a pig tractor doesn't need much. That's the point. We keep ours in an 8- x 10-foot pen framed of scrap lumber and light balsam poles cut from the woods. If the pen is much bigger, it grows unwieldy. There's no need to anchor it because the pen must be mobile.

Indeed the pig is mightier than the plow. As I rotate the pig tractor over sod or garden soil, the land is fertilized and tilled. Roots and stones are unearthed, and we clear them away. The pig gains weight and good health on idle land and, eventually, so do we. There's no hassle with manure handling, ventilation, barn building or fencing. One scavenger I know put together a pig pen of surplus bedsprings. Another linked fence panels with wire loops so he can maneuver the pen alone, lifting one side at a time. It's not important to build a gate. If I must go in, I climb the fence. For watering, we lower a bucket into a heavy wood frame so it's well anchored and easy to clean and refill.

A couple of points on pig tractor design. Space the fencing tight enough to keep the little pig from getting his head stuck. You'll hear about it if you don't. And make sure that the roof won't tip water back into his plot. A removable top allows for pitch adjustment on different slopes. Most of all, keep it lightweight. Ellen and I can easily lift the pen and move it the requisite 10 feet per trip, after we take down the convertible top.

The pig tractor doesn't guzzle expensive fuels, but he does need daily maintenance and water. We mix his grain 4:1 provender to soy meal and add a little powdered milk and kitchen scraps. For greens we grow him a row of swiss chard and add thinnings from the garden and the herb patch. We steer clear of medicated feeds and have yet to call the vet. When there's a surplus of eggs from the hens, the pig tractor gets his share. If we eat out, we always ask for a piggy bag for leftovers.

Altogether, I figure it costs about $125 for fuel, plus a little extra for the salt-and-maple-syrup brine and freezer paper. Figuring in the cost of the piglet, the total comes to roughly $165 or about a buck a pound.

Now the swineherd who sells us a pig every spring claims that he can raise a pig tractor for $50. "Leftovers, friend, that's where it's at!" Our swineherd is a master of recycling. Last year he named his pig Pepperoni. It grew on leftovers from the local pizzeria. In fact, he tells me there's a waiting list for scraps at neighborhood restaurants. But we're sticking with grain and vegetables. Who needs a carnivorous tractor? Look what happened to my neighbor, B. He fed his pig meat scraps. One day his favorite Muscovy duck took a walk down to the pig pen and never came back. Needless to say, the pig was off-limits to B's kids after that.

Ok, say you've got your pig tractor started and you're ready to plow. Nothing to it. To keep your engine chugging along, here are some techniques I've picked up. On a slope, always plow uphill. Each time you move ahead, set up the pig tractor with the roof and bed on the high end of the pen. At the opposite end, you'll see the pig set up his privy. Thus rainfall and manure runoff will stream downhill, behind. Your pig tractor will always have a clean garage.

To keep from flooding your engine, steer clear of waterways. But not *too* far. For efficient cooling it's best to run the pig tractor near a water source. Ours works best in a garden sited below the pond. Every year we rotate him through a fallow patch about a third the size of the garden, and the plot constantly thickens. His drinking water comes down by gravity flow through the same hose that irrigates the vegetables.

Over the growing season a pig tractor spreads several hundred pounds of manure. To improve the composting process, I layer the fresh manure with mulch hay every few days. This helps the manure break down in the soil without becoming impacted. It also keeps down flies and aroma. To save hay, I pitch old bedding into the pig privy. We drive the pig tractor slowly at the start, but by mid-season he's moving every week.

A well-oiled pig tractor runs smoothest. This summer, Pig Tractor III grew the smoothest hide and softest bristles in the valley because Ellen gave him a spring oiling. It was a polish of vegetable oil to prevent sunburn and an undercoat of pennyroyal oil to repel wood ticks and lice.

It's also possible to run chickens on the pig tractor principle, as a clever neighbor does. Instead of one hog in a pen, he's running ten hens in a cage without a floor. "It's third world agriculture," he says, "perfect for undeveloped countries like this part of Orange County." His chickens excel at weeding garden edges and preying on insect pests.

Traditionally, farmers often turn a few hogs loose in the corn field after harvest to uproot stalks, enrich the soil, and fatten up. A pig tractor does the same job, without running loose. It's also possible to grow fuel especially for the pig tractor, such as beets and turnips and mangels, and then drive him over the field to fill up.

Nothing about killing the tractor engine is easy, but the portable pen can help. We try to arrange plowing so the pig tractor winds up underneath the hanging tree, right beside the scalding tank, at butchering time. That way, after the bleed, he can be hoisted right out of the pen. Otherwise, we knock off a few boards to open up. But if the thought of slaughter turns you off, there's always a call for pig tractors on the hoof.

REGAL LAGER

Watered-down, freeze-dried, pumped up with CO_2, and filtered through asbestos—that's Twentieth-Century Beer. How easy it is these days to drown in bad taste.

"Fairy piss." That's how lumberjacks order today's thin commercial beers. And they drink it! Homebrew is the only way out.

But pity the poor cottage brewer: prone to creeping sloth (an occupational hazard) and to self-confessions that the stuff just doesn't justify all the fermenting and bottling mess-up. I confess that, up until a few months ago, I, too, was down on the old homebrew beer (even after writing a modestly successful booklet on the subject).

The problem seemed to be in the ingredients: canned syrups with a tinny taste. Canned syrup? A fatal shortcut, perhaps? Maybe I shouldn't have chucked out the rolling pin and the black patent malt. But even in the woods we like a little progress. Finally giving up on the tinned syrups, I let my brewing gear languish in a shroud of dust rolls beneath the gas refrigerator and spent unconscionable sums on imported German beer. Knowing that I could do better didn't overcome my reluctance to resume coarse-cracking malted grains.

Then one day a gift arrived: a box of exotic malts, canned and hopped extracts with English/Gaelic labels. I cooked up a crock right off, and two more the next day: light, dark, and stout. They worked, and after a month the caps came hissing off the finest beers I've bottled.

Mountmellnick, Ireland, is the home of the outfit that turns out these all-barley malts—mostly for the Guiness Brewery and a few pedigreed whiskey distilleries. Only a small portion of Mountmellnick products are extracted, hopped, and sold to homebrewers. Duane's Imports,* a homebrew supplier, discovered these malts a few years back and arranged to import them. They tape an envelope of the properly weighed and matched yeast to each can and christen it a "Brewing Pack." They offer to ship them anywhere in the world. Even if you

*Duane's Imports, P.O. Box 433, Hershey, PA 17033.

can't fathom the Gaelic on the label, these malts are sure to teach a homebrewer why lager spelled backwards is regal.

The prices vary according to the quantity ordered, ranging from a stiff $7 per single can (35 oz.) to a reasonable $4.34 per can when ordered in cases of twelve. (Your choice of any proportion of light, dark, and stout.) Shipping by UPS is free to any destination in the continental U.S., with different surcharges added for mailing elsewhere. Duane's also offers a couple of "American" beers, hopped, with no additives, as well as a complete stock of paraphernalia, including their own *Home Brewing Handbook.*

But it's their exclusive license to deal Mountmellnick malts that sets Duane's ahead of the pack. Two suggestions: try brewing these malts without sugar, especially the light, for crystal clear beer. And write, don't call, Duane's. They keep the number secret. As the boss says, "When your customers are in varying stages of drunkenness at all hours, it's just something you have to do."

BORN-AGAIN VEGETABLES

Three vegetable gardens, a patch of herbs, a spreading orchard, a bed of blueberries, and a field of raspberries and blackberries—when people first see this place, the question is bound to be asked:

"Isn't it a lot of work?"

The answer is yes. There are days in the thick of the growing season when the carrots need thinning and the potato bugs need zapping and everything aches for water. That's when visions of white blankets of murderous frost dance in my head. Or at least that's how I used to feel, before I discovered some shortcut crops that help trim garden overtime. Now instead of growing everything under the sun, I relax a little. While the neighbors are out raising plastic cloches in the spring mud, Ellen and I dig into a fresh salad. Friends are likely to be planting in the middle of a gale while we're adding greens to an omelette. Where the food comes from is just outside our kitchen door.

About ten days after the snow disappears, roughly May Day here in the North, the first crop is up. Dandelions. Pity the folk who consider the "Lion's Tooth" a nuisance weed. After the marathon Vermont winter, a feast of fresh dandelion greens is survival medicine. We eat the greens fresh in salads or cooked with a slice of homegrown bacon. Raw, the taste is sharp, refreshing, almost like quinine. Cooked, it's milder. In a half-cup of cooked dandelion greens we are getting three times the Vitamin C and 20 times the Vitamin A waiting in an equivalent helping of cooked carrots, for instance. Not bad for a weed.

A portion of our dandelion crop comes up wild in the garden, and I yank the plants by their root, weeding and harvesting in one motion. The boiled root tastes a bit like an artichoke heart, but it's a nuisance to peel. The roasted root can be powdered to brew an ersatz coffee, but we leave that alone and are content with the greens. Elsewhere, most of the dandelion crop grows scattered about the two-acre clearing around the house. I leave these roots intact so we can have greens again next year.

The harvest opens in the sunniest spots and moves down into the cool shady hollows as spring ripens. It's important to track the young dandelions and to harvest before the flowers emerge and the greens grow too bitter. Our dandelion season extends to the end of May, when the clearing lights up like a galaxy of suns. I celebrate the end of harvest by gathering a pail of the golden flowers and brewing a gallon of dandelion wine.

On the heels of the early dandelions comes spinach—and we haven't yet touched a spade since last fall. The trick is to plant a row or two late in the preceding summer. In this region (zone 4) I've found that mid-August is about right. The idea is to start the crop about a month before the first frost. Come autumn, the spinach will die back and then sprout reborn in spring. It's important to choose a rich location with ample early spring sun. I don't plant in the middle of the garden so that it fouls up springtime tilling. Spinach winters over best if the roots lie insulated under snow. To help guarantee its comeback, I mulch the spinach under six inches of hay and peel it back in the spring.

Meanwhile, in the herb garden, Ellen is clipping chives to add an oniony zip to the dandelion and spinach salad that's forming. This hardy perennial is easy to start from seed or root division and it likes full sun. For best eating, the green tops should be snipped before developing purple flowers. If you crave extra spice, add garlic chives to the patch.

Our born-again spring crops are not limited to salad greens. A 20-foot row of parsnips planted last May turns into 20 pounds of sweet roots this spring. Kin to the carrot and celery, the parsnip is a vegetable born for the North. The roots contain about 18 percent carbohydrate, in starch, during the summer. While we are out skiing, the starch changes into sugar. In spring the ground thaws and the parsnips lie in storage, waiting to be uprooted and baked or put into soup.

I've learned to harvest the parsnip before spring advances too far along; otherwise, the roots spend energy making seed, and the plant tastes like balsa wood. I start off pulling as many as we need for the moment, right out of the ground. Once I see the green tops sprout more than an inch, I harvest the whole crop and pack it in peat moss down in the root cellar (which is cooler than the garden soil). The only problem with parsnips is that they are *too* sweet. By the end of May we are likely to have a surplus and no takers among our neighbors. That's when the roots make one last transformation. The parsnip contains enough natural sugar to produce a fine dry wine, without the addition of extra sweetener.

Parsley is another crop that winters-over well in the North. Like many early spring plants, it yields rich amounts of Vitamins A, B, and C. I've found that this biennial comes back strongest when planted in mid-summer. Late planting seems to ensure vigorous second year growth as well as a longer picking season before the plants go to seed. Spring rebirth is enhanced by a layer of insulating mulch applied in autumn, and parsley should be given a place of its own where it won't interfere with tilling.

In addition to the dandelions and the spring come-back crops, I've come to savor a couple of mid-season wild edibles: lamb's quarters and milkweed. Known also as pigweed or wild amaranth, lamb's quarters packs heavy charges of vitamins. We mix the greens in salads or cook them like spinach. They grow almost exclusively in the garden. Instead of weeding them out entirely, I allow the plants to stand wherever they don't crowd other crops. I'm careful to permit a bunch to go to seed so we can welcome them back again next year. Milkweed lovers boast that everything about the plant is edible: shoots, flowers, and pods. I've tried them all and it's the flowers that I favor, just before they pop open. I boil the flowers briefly, drain off the first water, add fresh water, and boil again. Changing the water flushes away the slightly bitter taste. I know the milkweed is ready when the purple flowers turn green in the pot. With a little butter melted on top, this is a dish to stay home for.

Asparagus and rhubarb are the classic perennials. Once established, they'll return each spring as sure as Canada geese. And if you are lucky enough to discover a patch of fiddlehead ferns, keep it quiet. Few springtime treasures are so sought after or as tasty.

I could add more labor-saving crops to the list, and gardening books and wild-food guides are stuffed with them. But there's no sense in overdoing—the idea is to make less work for yourself, not more.

CRITTERS IN THE CROPS

It was a hot summer for varmints. One fat raccoon had two square miles of Orange County in a lather. He polished off a garden full of green beans, a strawberry patch, and two and a half turkeys, yanked off their perch and pulled through the lath floor one bite after another. That was enough to spur three families to band together and buy a Havahart trap. They threw a victory celebration the night they lured the coon into the steel cage and drowned it in the brook. But who chewed up all the celery two nights later?

I heard about another raid. I met a friend at an art gallery. "You're looking pale for such a sunny summer," I said. It was opening night and I watched the wine glass in his hand flap like the flag on Mt. Washington. He told me that his garden had been ravaged by a woodchuck. No sooner would the seeds sprout than they'd be leveled. "But I got him," he said. "This morning." My pal, who never shot anything bigger than an 8 x 10 view camera, told me he'd borrowed a .44 magnum rifle from a neighbor. He set up a stakeout in a second-story window overlooking the garden. Then he got up at dawn, waited, and when the woodchuck showed he fired. "I hit him but he wasn't dead. So I ran down the stairs and out to the garden and he was still twitching. I had to shoot him point blank. I could feel the adrenalin zapping through me like lightning. Have you ever seen what a .44 magnum can do? It's enough to make you go back to shopping at Grand Union."

To console my friend I told him about the summer I started raising birds. One night a screeching chicken woke me up. It was pitch dark. The cry was so awful I jumped out of bed and raced to the chicken house buck naked, howling like a banshee. I wanted to scare it off, but I felt just as terrified as that chicken. Imagine a bear! But it was a coon, and he'd chewed a wing off Flyer, my favorite hen. She was still alive. Ellen brought out the cleaver and finished her off by flashlight. That night I learned forever to shut the chicken house door. The coon got away.

Perhaps these skirmishes have a familiar ring. It's not often that a grower can fend off predators without brute force. But once in a while there's a breakthrough. The latest happened down at our pond. For several years Ellen and I have been raising trout, which we share with an arrogant kingfisher. The fish must make an appetizing sight from above. When the rainbows jump for flies the pond looks like a skillet full of exploding popcorn. Luckily, on arrival, the kingfisher sounds his own air raid alarm. It's a wild cackle loud as castanets. Too bad he doesn't schedule his performances in the evening, or better yet, a matinee. Then it would be easy enough to trot down to the pond and chuck a few rotten tomatoes. Instead, his rattle greets the summer dawn, and I stumble out of bed, skid on the dewy grass and run around the shore yelling at a bird. It's a hell of a way to start the day. But what's the alternative? The kingfisher is a wild migratory waterfowl, protected by federal law, so you can't shoot him. And covering the pond with protective netting would be expensive and awkward. I tried raising an aquacultural scarecrow—a giant koi kite waving on a pole—but it only seemed to whet his appetite.

So my spirits took a nose dive—till the Fourth of July. The kingfisher roused me from dreams of Roman Candles. Something clicked. Ellen had a box of bottle rockets in the closet!

I threw off the sheets and plucked out a few rockets. I grabbed some matches and an empty Molson's bottle. I stepped out on the porch. The sun was rising and a light mist drifted over the water. I slid a Whistling Moon Traveler into the bottle, lit the fuse, and aimed. The fuse sparkled. The rocket ignited. Screeching like a stuck pig, it shot out toward the pond. In a flash it was arcing over the shore showering smoke and sparks. Over the middle of the pond the rocket exploded.

The kingfisher shrieked and flew. Later I went for a swim and retrieved the floating casing. The kingfisher doesn't come around much anymore. But if he does, I send him a reminder of Independence Day.

QUALITY IS A 50-YEAR-OLD GAS-BURNING REFRIGERATOR (NOT FOR SALE)

I know: "They don't make 'em like they used to" sounds like a curmudgeon's view of our world of plastics and 2.5 mph car bumpers, and, besides, it's just not cool to yearn for the good old days. So let me just ask, why are so many people scrambling to buy my 50-year-old Servel gas refrigerator?

After all, LP dealers are selling brand-new gas coolers. Why is it that my 1930s Servel has the aura of an antique Wurlitzer Juke Box? Every time I invite someone up for dinner on the hill, one look in the kitchen and I've got another tempting offer. One fellow even wrote me a check right here in the house. I tore it up. But sometimes I wonder. Maybe I should use the money to buy a decent truck. Why not? I'd still have a root cellar to keep food chilled. Trouble is, the root cellar is 30 paces from the house, and you can get drenched just going for the butter. On the other hand, the Servel sits right in the kitchen cooking up a steady 40 degrees, even in July's top heat. And after a sizzling day of banging nails and swatting black flies, an icy ale from the fridge is carbonated Nirvana.

When I say cooking, I'm not kidding. The Servel burns liquid propane gas to cool. The "motor" works more like an oven.

It's tucked down low under the refrigeration compartment. A flame jets out under a sealed container that heats up an ammonia refrigerant. As the solution gasifies it circulates through a coiled piping system withdrawing the heat around it—the absorption effect it's called—and thus it cools.

An electric refrigerator works on a similar principle, but the refrigerant is gasified by the compression of an electric pump. In the refrigerator wars, electric beats gas because it appears most efficient. There's hardly any heat rising underneath the chest to counteract the cooling. (At least it looks efficient until you start counting up the drawbacks of electricity where it's generated, often at a loss of efficiency that exceeds the Servel.) However, where there's no electricity—right here, for instance—the gas refrigerator wins. I suppose that's why so many people in the country want one. Why they don't make 'em like they used to is anybody's guess. Perhaps it's because most new gas refrigerators are built for recreational vehicles, and they're small, poorly insulated, and expensive.

On the other hand, the Servel is a full-size cooler—about seven cubic feet, including a freezer box. Built during the Thirties by the Servel Corporation of Evansville, Indiana, it was modeled on a Swedish design. LP gas fueled the cooling system, with no moving parts except the door. This was a big improvement over the smelly, temperamental kerosene refrigerators of the time, like the Tru Kold and Icy Ball. Servels became popular in rural areas, known for their reliability and silence. Later, with the advent of rural electrification following World War II, demand for fuel-burning coolers dropped and the company closed. But the Servels kept right on freezing, maintenance free. The only sign of age on this one is a slightly worn door gasket, and the designers anticipated that with an adjustable door latch. The designers also froze in the look of their era, the art deco Thirties. French curves soften the corners, and streamlined contours embossed on the door add an old-fashioned Futurist effect. After dark when the gas jet at the base glows fiery blue, the Servel looks like Flash Gordon's rocket blasting off. In a backwoods kitchen on a hot summer night there's not a cooler sight.

BLACKBERRY VERITAS

When I think of August, I see the evening sun pouring through the kitchen door warm and red. It filters through the screen and the mesh lights up like hot coals. The kitchen feels tropical: sweet and steamy. As the sunlight runs up the back wall it glints off a stout glass crock, fades and disappears. Now sit still and listen close . . . . There's no mistaking it: the sizzle and sputter of fermenting wine.

Around home, August means wild berry wine. Red raspberries, black raspberries, and mostly the sweet and thorny blackberry. Last summer I made five gallons of the blackberry brew. Each gallon has its own character: the young and sharp first pressing; the sweeter mid-August wine, and the conclusive spirits, strong and spicy. Perhaps you've tasted vintages of red grape wine that suggest the flavor of blackberries, Zinfandel for instance. Our blackberry wines will remind you of no grape wine you've tried, although some friends detect an echo of fine sherry.

Odds are you've never tasted berry wine, wild or tame. Traditionally, wine made from anything but grapes is disdained thoroughly. It's called *false* and the appellation "wine" only a courtesy. This snobbery stems from a long-standing grape lovers' quarrel with vintners who beefed up the alcohol content of their wine, or diluted it, using the fermented juice of some common fruit or vegetable. A favorite was elderberry juice, used to top off barrels of port. Now, as a consequence, wine is legally bound to come from the grape. The fermented juice of other crops must be labeled: cider, saki, arrack, and so on. Never mind that sugar is permitted to be added to grape wine, to the dismay of "true" wine lovers.

Indeed, sugar is the modern wine maker's elderberry: the low-budget short-cut. It's not surprising that sugar turned up in my first crock of blackberry wine. Virtually every blackberry wine recipe I've read recommends adding sugar, generally in this proportion: three pounds berries, one gallon water, and two pounds sugar—plus, of course, yeast.

The wine turned out decent enough, but I couldn't help wonder if the sugar hadn't cheapened it. There was a cloying sweetness, something a shade . . . false. I could feel my prejudices rising. Years ago, making beer, I'd learned that there's no comparison between an all-malt brew and one concocted with malt and sugar. The Germans agree. Germany is one country in the world where brewing beer with sugar is *verboten*. We all know the result: German beer is heads above the rest.

But what would I use instead? Why not take a hint from the bees making their own nectar from the berries: a silky Vermont honey to brew a truly wild wine. I had plenty of clover honey on hand, best for wine making because of its mild flavor. The only missing ingredient was wine yeast. After a quick search under the kitchen sink, I nabbed a dusty packet of lager yeast. They say adversity can bring out the best in people: why not wine? I tore open the yeast and pitched it into the crock. After the primary fermentation died down, I siphoned off the brew into quart bottles, added a bit of extra honey for spritz, and riveted on the caps. Then I showed a bottle to Ellen.

"Blackberry beer?" she asked, sounding doubtful.

I reminded her of the *Berlinerweiser*. That's a stein full of cold lager laced with cherry syrup. First time I saw one I was appalled. But it wasn't bad. Good for coughs, too.

We opened the first bottles at Thanksgiving. A little early for properly aged wine, but just right for beer. It was a hit.

"Like champagne and blackberry pie," Ellen decided.

We named it fruit beer.

After that, I knew my wine making had nowhere to go but up. Over the years I dropped the fruit beer, but stuck with the blackberries and honey. I've refined a wine recipe that's delicious and simple. After all, blackberry wine making dovetails with the humongous harvests of August, and who's got time for capping quarts?

THE RECIPE

Before you start picking, stock up on wine-making basics. You'll need a clean two-gallon glass or ceramic crock for the primary fermenter; a hydrometer to float in your brew and tell you its density, and thus the alcohol content (potential at the start, and finished); a sieve and some cheesecloth for straining; a plastic siphon tube; and two one-gallon glass jugs.

You'll also need these ingredients for each gallon of wine: two or three pounds of honey, depending on the desired strength of the wine and the sweetness of the berries. A packet of Montrachet wine yeast. One gallon of good spring water (chlorinated tap water is *verboten*). And a solid three pounds of fresh-picked, ripe, wild blackberries. In a pinch you can use domesticated but the flavor just won't measure up to wild. (A tablespoon of fresh-squeezed lemon juice will give the wine a little extra tang, especially in the case of domestic berries, but I don't use it.)

Pour the berries into the crock and crush. I like using a stainless steel potato masher. Now pour over the berries one gallon of freshly boiled spring water. Stir, cover, and let sit overnight. After 24 hours, pour in two pounds of honey and dissolve by stirring. Check starting gravity and add more honey if desired. Specific gravity should be between 1.080 and 1.095, depending on your taste. The more honey, the stronger the wine, although it will also be sweeter. Add a packet of Montrachet wine yeast, and stir. (Remember that wine ferments best between 50 and 70 degrees.) Cover and let this ferment for five to six days, stirring once a day. Now strain out the fruit pulp using the sieve lined with cheesecloth, and press to get the juice out. Siphon the wine into the gallon jugs. You will have one full gallon, plus a small amount in the other. Cover loosely. I use wax paper held on with a rubber band. The object is to allow the bubbling CO_2 to escape, but to let no bugs in. After about three weeks, siphon off the juice into clean wine bottles, leaving all sediment behind, and cork. Age for a year—or at least till Christmas.

GOBBLERS AND GOOBERS

It was not a banner year: The town doubled our taxes and my favorite calico cat got eaten by a red fox. But the gobblers came through with flying colors. It's amazing how a tender, homegrown bird improves the flavor of tough times.

It takes a lot more than money to raise gobblers as good as these. What it takes (a bow to my wife Ellen for making the discovery) is a lot of heart. Peanut hearts, to be precise. That and a daily salad of garden greens, both thinnings and custom-grown. In the spring I plant an extra row of swiss chard and turnips for the turkeys. We keep the roots, they get the greens.

This astounds our neighbors. The local view is that turkeys are stupid and that they like to stand around in the rain and catch blackhead disease. Growers talk about watching healthy birds croak for no clear reason. *Turkey.* Say the word and you conjure up a calamity. There is some truth to all this but it doesn't help explain how millions of the birds land dead center on American holiday tables. Perhaps the gobbler is a bird of paradox. The paradox is that a bird resembling a prehistoric Pterodactyl could not only survive in the Space Age, it actually thrives. A bird synonymous with failure is relished by the richest citizens on the planet. A bird notoriously difficult to keep alive sells for less per pound than a hardy hog. "A bird to forget," as one farming handbook warns.

I disagree. I also admit I'm not a turkey man, professionally. What I offer, beyond the recommendation of my taste buds, is four years of experience: a total of 19 birds. The hens have ranged from 10 to 18 pounds, the toms from 10 to 29. The average weight fell over the past couple of years, but now it's climbing again.

After dressing off the first crop—five birds, average weight 25 pounds—we quit feeding the birds "medicated turkey grower pellets." That was when the birds shrunk. Why fiddle with success? Over the years I'd been watching the evidence mount against "modern meat." Commercial livestock feed is usually laced with preservatives, antibiotics and sometimes hormones. This makes it possible to grow critters in crowded, often unclean conditions, and to grow them fast. For the pharmacy-farmer, the profits can be big. For the people who eat the meat, who knows? It's no secret that many preservatives are carcinogenic. Residual antibiotics can lower natural resistance to disease. Hormones confuse the glands. The ingredients label on a sack of medicated turkey grower pellets reads like a chemistry exam.

Q. Define 4-Nitrophenylarsonic acid.

A. Arsenic.

How about Dried Streptomyces Fermentation Residue? According to Dr. Marvin W. Colburn, a nutritionist at Blue Seal Feeds in Lawrence, Massachusetts, it's a source of "unidentified growth factors" in their feeds. And Ethoxyquin? (A preservative.) The list goes on.

I remember the proprietor of the feed store who listened to Ellen's first request for unmedicated feed, and replied, "Scared you'll grow a moustache?" The room was packed with customers and he got some laughs. That was before the newspapers began headlining stories about Puerto Rican children growing breasts at age three. Girls and boys. Puerto Rican children eat a lot of chicken, and thereby, a lot of hormones. In Puerto Rico, until recently, there had been no limits on feed hormone levels. Levels in the U.S. are regulated and are lower. Still, there is a growing market for unmedicated "organic" meat and fowl.

We switch off the medicated starter after our turkeys have gone through one 100-pound bag, which is about seven weeks for five birds. That first bag is a bow to science, and we are grateful for the preventive medicine. Young poults—motherless, remember, and nearly featherless—are vulnerable to disease. But after a few weeks these are plucky birds. They've trouped from the brooder shed to the backyard pen. After that, if you treat them right, there's no call for medicated feed. Supply fresh water every day, and greens right from the start. Dandelion greens and clover leaves are early favorites, up before the garden crops; they should be shredded while the birds are still young. A clean environment is needed, too: fresh litter every day in the brooder, and later, in the turkey house, a wood slat floor to let the manure fall through.

For awhile we followed the starter feed with oats and cracked corn (scratch feed) and plenty of greens on the side. The birds were very healthy on this—and very lean. After 18 weeks our biggest tom dressed out at ten pounds, including giblets. He looked like a plucked partridge. Not a sign of fat. He was pure indeed, what there was of him. Considering all the time we had spent tending the young poults—the stove fires to stoke in the brooder shed, the fresh bedding and water each day—it seemed like a meager return, those ten-pound birds, organic or not.

Then an encouraging ad turned up in the local paper that autumn: "20–30 pound Organic Turkeys." Ellen called the farmer. "What makes them organic?" she asked.

"We don't feed them medicated turkey feed," he answered. "We use 15 percent dairy ration, the same grain pellets I feed my Holsteins."

True, according to the dairy-ration feed label there were no antibiotics. But there were preservatives and vague by-products similar to those in commercial turkey feed. So his turkeys didn't impress us. But the 15 percent protein count did. Corn we had been using contained a slight 8 percent.

That winter Ellen heard a story about a Georgia peanut farmer who raised turkeys on surplus nuts. It wasn't clear how soon he started the gobblers on the goobers, or how great a percentage they amounted to in the feed, but it seemed like a good idea. This lowly legume, known to some as the "goober pea," develops its seeds underground; hence it's also called the "ground nut." It packs some of the highest food levels of any vegetable, rivalling soybeans in protein and exceeding soy in the B vitamins and fat. Unfortunately, at $3 a pound, it also seemed an expensive idea. I asked the fellow at the grain store how on earth people could afford it.

"They must be nuts," he grumbled. But he said he would see what he could dig up. A few days later we checked back. For $30 he would sell us 100 pounds of peanut "*hearts*."

Later I learned that the hearts are separated during the making of peanut butter and peanut candy. People find that the hearts have a bitter taste. Turkeys don't mind. We ordered a bag in the spring and picked up five white turkey poults.

When the birds came off their starter feed and onto their peanut hearts it was love at first sight. Twenty weeks after bringing them home we dressed them out: average 20 pounds. The total cost was $100: $10 for the poults, $90 for the starter feed, grain and goobers. That comes to about $1.25 a pound. Around here, the price for locally grown "organic" turkeys runs about $1.75 per pound, when they can be found at all. In New York City, they sell for as much as $10 a pound.

For all interested in raising goober-fed gobblers, a few hints. We begin feeding the hearts as soon as our four or five birds have polished off their first 100-pound bag of "Medicated Crumbles." At 24 percent protein and a whopping 42 percent fat, the tiny hearts, small as radish seed, add weight to the birds fast. We supplement the hearts with dandelion greens, clover leaves and garden greens, mix in soy meal, for extra plant protein, and cracked corn for grain energy. The ratio is about 50 percent goobers.

It's important not to use peanut hearts as the only feed. This was emphasized by both Dr. Colburn and Dr. Richard M. Lockwood of Lockwood Feed Service, a specialty feed ingredients supplier in Newton, Massachusetts. Dr. Lockwood explained that "there are limitations in feeding only peanut hearts in a turkey finishing diet. It is low in lysine." Soybean meal and corn will balance that. "Because of the high oil content, you run the risk of having a negative effect on the carcass, leading to soft fat." He explained that because of the high fat content, it is important that the hearts be fresh, and that they be stored in a cool, dry place. Dr. Colburn said that storage life is about six months in winter and two months in summer. If the hearts don't smell right or are musty, they are rancid and should not be used."

A little extra vigilance, plus some shredded four-leaf clovers for luck, doesn't seem a bad exchange for a flock of pure, tender peanut butterballs.

WOODS

SHARECROPPING THE TOPS (or FOREST GLADIATOR)

Sharecropping is a word that conjures up dust bowl ballads, *The Grapes of Wrath*, and poor tenant farmers who pay their rent slaving for a landowner. But on my woodlot it's simply another form of barter: lumber for labor. It's particularly well-suited to the forest where there's enough stumpage to trade for the timber harvest, as well as fill the owner's woodshed. I like it especially because there's no capital expense. For the "land poor" it can mean the difference between harvesting your resources and watching them rot.

Last autumn's firewood harvest is a good example of forest sharecropping. As usual, the objective was to get the wood down (cutting is the easy part; the challenge is getting the wood home). My 45-acre woodlot covers the hilltop east of the house, and gravity is king. Gravity takes down the trees after they're chopped, and helps the horses pull them downhill over the snow. I should add that the bulliest woodlot is of little value to the sharecropper if it lies *below* the homestead or roadside landing. Logging is marginal enough these days, and the prospect of hauling trees uphill is likely to discourage a woodsman working for just a cut of the crop.

Selective thinning is the rule here, and the goal is a continually regenerating crop of trees. According to a rough rule of thumb, a healthy forest will produce at least a cord of thinnings per acre per year. Over nine years, I've never taken out that much. Nonetheless, I've traded softwood stumpage for most of the lumber I used to build the house and studio; I've sold a truckload or two a year of soft and hardwood to pay taxes (roughly the equivalent of 5000 board feet); and every year I get down enough firewood to keep the main house and two outbuildings warm, with enough surplus to sharecrop with a woodsman.

The crop to get down was mostly rock maple tops, with a scattering of white birch. More than a year before, I had thinned out the hilltop sugar bush, cutting the leaners, canopy crowders, and bad gizzards. Instinctively I undercut, and I don't mean simply notching. I limited the harvest to two truckloads. It's tough to predict the scalping each load will take, so I cut slow to conserve.

Slow going also conserves loggers. That's why I favor horses over machines. Not that you can't get run over by a timber hitch or stomped on by a one-ton Belgian. It's just that there's more time to get out of the way, which is helpful when you're bushed and the footing is greasy; and in logging, whether by horse or diesel, that's usually the case.

Slow going, of course, has its drawbacks. That's why I was in a hurry last Halloween to cinch the deal with my pal, Tofer. There was enough wood on the shed floor to get to Christmas; barring any below-zero marathons, maybe New Year's. But I knew I'd need that dry wood to coax along the greener logs coming in. Technically I was out of wood. Fortunately, so was Tofer.

Tofer Sharp is a baker by trade, but he moonlights with a pair of Belgians. He's tall, sandy haired and loose, with a kind of detached manner that must be right for those sunny days when you have to hang around inside waiting for 100 loaves of bread to rise.

I agreed to board Frank and Jeanette here, and Tofer planned to commute to the woods. We built a shelter for the horses in back of the cabin, and Tofer strung a battery powered electric fence for a corral. Then he trucked up a load of hay; we stacked the bales outside the corral, and covered them with a tarp. It looked like a good partnership.

Tofer would supply the hay and grain and drive the horses, and I'd supply the tops. We figured on splitting the wood three to one in Tofer's favor. I'd take care of the horses when Tofer went home, and rake in a ton of manure for the garden.

Southbound geese laced the skies the morning Tofer hitched Frank and Jeanette to his wagon and drove them up the mountain. He introduced the horses to their new home and clipped the fence to a six-volt battery. The transformer was nailed to a maple tree. Plunk . . . plunk . . . it pulsed like an amplified sap bucket in spring.

Before long we had a path beaten between the pond and the corral. Tofer complimented me on the water.

"Frank's very particular. Usually in a strange place he won't touch a drop for days."

Frank had his nose buried in the bucket, and I could see the water going down in one-gallon gulps. Over the next four weeks I hauled upwards of 60 gallons a day, depending on Tofer's schedule. I often wished Frank didn't like the water quite so much.

Frank is a strawberry roan Belgian, about 1600 pounds. Like most geldings, he works hard and has a friendly, somewhat sluggish disposition. Jeanette's another story. Tofer had just weaned her first-born, an eight-week-old mare named Poppy. I think Poppy was one of the reasons Tofer jumped at the sharecropping deal. He needed a place out of earshot of the colt to ease the weaning. Consequently, Jeanette's udder was full, and on top of that she was bred again. Besides, she's Quebecois. In the process of drying her out and teaching gee and haw with a Vermont accent, Tofer damn near got his head kicked in.

Most days—between baking—Tofer arrived about nine. By then I had the horses fed and watered, so he would harness up and go to work. It was hunting season, so I tied red ribbons to the horse collars. That was a lot easier than posting 45 acres and it didn't rub anybody the wrong way. Around here, post your land and you're asking for a range war. The ribbons looked glorious, harking back to the days when Belgians like Frank and Jeanette carried knights in iron armour, colors flashing.

"Horses insured?" I asked.

"Just fire and theft."

Tofer started out skidding solo with Frank. That made it easier for Jeanette, I suppose, but she would have preferred working to being alone. Nonetheless, it was a long draw, about 1/5 mile, and it made better sense to yard the tops at the pinnacle and then bring down big hitches with the team. As soon as the wood started coming down, I got to work cutting, splitting, stacking.

Sometimes I went into the woods to help. I carried up the come-along to pull out tops that were hung up. I cleared trails. But mostly I hiked up just to watch. I've worked with horse loggers before, but I've never seen anyone with a style like Tofer's. When he skids out a hitch, he never lets loose of the reins. He keeps pace with the horses, trotting along on a trail or galloping down the mountain. His reins extend about 10 feet behind the team, so he takes position to one side of the hitch (usually the uphill side), clicks his tongue and takes off.

Tofer has developed certain techniques that enable him to adapt to turns of the trail and changes in terrain. If an obstacle looms up on his side of the hitch, he may hop up on the log and ride it like a slalom ski. Or if he meets a tree on his side, he'll keep to the outside and pass the reins from one hand to the other, around the tree. On a downhill trail that takes a switchback, he jumps up on the log and after the turn he steps off on the other side, back on the uphill slope. On a steep and slippery trail with the turns coming fast, Tofer zigzags down the mountain like a lightning bolt. This is not the recommended teamster's style. It's the style of the north country gladiator.

There's no denying the pleasure of falling asleep to the thump of night-walking Belgians, but sharecropping has its nightmares, too. One day I butchered a pig inside the house because Tofer wouldn't allow it outdoors. He had heard that the smell of fresh blood might induce Jeanette to abort. Actually, I suspect that Tofer, a vegetarian, wanted to get himself off the hook, not Jeanette.

By Thanksgiving I had all the wood I needed, and so did Tofer. I helped him load his truck six or seven times, a solid ten cords. I'll never forget the last load, one evening after sunset. The old Ford smoked and roared like a dragon, but it just wouldn't back up. Every time Tofer eased up on the clutch and gunned it, the six-wheeler just hopped back a step and the engine died, or backfired, and he had to pounce on the clutch and the brake and start again. Tofer tried over and over, but he wound up losing ground, rolling closer and closer to the pond.

The truck was loaded with monster maple, and the wooden sides bulged and strained against the binding chains. I stood on the dam and watched Tofer try to coax the Ford up the slope to the road. The truck was overloaded and the spark plugs were probably gummed. But the headlights on the water glowed alarmingly bright. Tofer revved the engine hard, and the hills echoed back as loud as a herd of Jerseys in heat. I knew if he didn't make it this time, the truck was going in.

"Go!" I shouted.

The truck jumped forward an instant, rolled back, hesitated as the engine skipped a beat and then screamed up the bank. I watched Tofer roll down the road till he disappeared in the dark.

BORROWED SCENERY

When I settled here there was nothing but trees. So I cut a clearing for the house and moved out from there. I cut most extensively to the south to bring in the sun. But the dramatic views lay to the northwest, obscured by a grove of balsams: a 900-acre Vermont state forest chockablock full of hardwoods and coyotes; Invisible Pond, folded secretly into the watershed (the only giveaway the plumes of rising morning mist); and crowning all, a mountain often shrouded in clouds or snow. The mountain cliffs caught the sunrise and held the tinted sky at dusk.

I glimpsed this view from the hill looming behind the house, and longed to bring it in. The easy way to gain the overlook would have been to fell the balsams. But I had misgivings. The wave of trees obstructed the long-distance view, but it also protected me from the north wind. Besides that, the thick evergreens formed a natural fence between me, the road, and the neighbors. I looked again. Imagining the view from the porch, I saw that only the top ten feet or so of each tree seemed to block the way. Perhaps if I topped a dozen or so I'd have a good part of the view and the protection of the shelter belt, too. So I went at it, scaling one tree at a time, saw in hand, until I'd lopped off a clearing 40 feet over the forest floor. Then I returned home and turned north. I looked through a notch that lined up with the mountain like a gunsight. Now as the seasons roll by, so does the view through my evergreen window. And when I prune back the trees, the frame changes just enough to give the view a refreshing new slant.

Autumn is tops for pruning, best of all a frosty morning when the sap's stopped weeping and hot colors blaze on the horizon. How steadily these evergreens ascend. Even as I go up and cut they're growing still. I look forward to a fiery view when I get home.

The pleasure of having the trees and view, too, has been magnified by a recent discovery. Unknowingly, I've been practicing a classical Japanese gardening technique. It's called *shakkei*—borrowed scenery—and it's been a tradition in temple gardens since the early seventeenth century.

Now as anyone who ever assumed the lotus position will know, Japanese temple gardens, with their Buddhist roots, were (and continue to be) places for peacefulness and meditation, not vegetables. Enlightenment is the crop, and the plot is likely to be a symbolic composition of sand and stones in an enclosed area that screens out unwanted visual distractions and physical intrusions. Barriers are important, especially evergreens. Yet the garden should not feel confining. In fact, invariably there is some visual link between the garden and the world beyond. Hence the *shakkei* tradition.

The temple garden of Entsuji, in Kyoto, is noted for its striking use of borrowed scenery. Here's how it's described by Mitchell Bring and Josse Wayembergh, in their book *Japanese Gardens: Design and Meaning*.

> The low hedge along the rear of the garden . . . acts as the lower part of the frame that includes Mt. Hiei as borrowed scenery, making it part of the garden composition. Some tall cypress and pine trees stand close to the hedge. The lower edge of their foliage forms the upper part of a frame enclosing the view of the mountain. The tree trunks form the sides of the frame and create a middle ground that draws the mountain into the composition.

Unlike Mt. Hiei, the mountain scene I captured lacks the upper horizontal frame, although on special occasions a cumulus cloud fills the gap. Otherwise my view seems like an eerie echo of *shakkei* technique. Yet I imagine few Japanese gardeners would be surprised. To them, the landscape is the greatest teacher.

A WOODLOT HARVEST

If there had been any doubts about a timber harvest, they vanished as the year came to an end. I'd never seen the evergreens sprout such a heavy crop of cones. From a distance you'd imagine the forest was blighted and dying. But it was a brown shroud of fat seed cones cloaking the trees. According to a naturalist at the Vermont Institute of Natural Science, it was the biggest seed crop in memory, which helped explain why the birds were ignoring the feeders. Those plump cones also signaled a good year for chopping: they were the seeds for a new forest.

It would mean the end of a landmark grove. Several spruce measured three feet through at the butt and towered over the nearby deciduous trees. From the other side of the valley the giant spruce looked like a wave cresting the ridge. But when you looked closer there were signs of crowding and decay: uprooted trees, broken tops, cracked trunks, bleeding gum. A good thinning would mean the start of a vigorous new stand. And a fine timber pile on the knoll in front of my house. I began to imagine the barn I needed rising in a corner of the clearing.

My woodlot straddles a 45-acre ridge of mixed hard and softwoods, and I work the harvests in a patchwork fashion. Sometimes I'll cut firewood and hire a neighbor to help haul it out; sometimes I'll sharecrop a few truckloads of timber with a logger. That way, there's a guaranteed annual crop. Small harvests insure against the kind of wipeout that strikes woodlot owners who cut all their assets in one swoop. The problem with small harvests is that it may be difficult to entice a logger with just a couple of truckloads, say 10,000 board feet. When you're burdened with $500 a week in payments on a skidder and a 16-wheeler, it's not worth setting up a new lot for less than a truckload or two each day. The way around this, I've found, is to work with a horse logger. The pace is slow (good insurance against over-cutting) and the horse logger's lower "equipment" costs mean he can turn a profit on a smaller cut. I've had loggers truck the team in and out every day, or board the horses here. But the best deal is working with a logger who lives close by; he can ride his sled up in the morning and home at dusk. And so I asked Ralph Coutermarsh to cut the spruce. He lives a mile down the road, and he's one of the most experienced horse loggers around. He wasn't a bit reluctant to tackle these limby evergreens. Another logger I spoke to

glanced at one burly spruce and snarled, "I'd rather go to prison than cut that octopus!" As it turned out, just limbing the tree emptied a full chain saw tank.

We marked the trees together. I showed Ralph the trees I thought were ripe to go, he showed me the ones he *knew*. As the cutting began he'd bet me that one tree or another would be rotten. Some of them looked fine outside. The chain saw screeched, the tree boomed in the snow. Damned if the butt wasn't rotten inside.

"That's what a lifetime of chopping teaches," Ralph said.

Ralph's son came along and did most of the chain sawing. His name is Ralph, Jr., but everybody calls him Bozo. He's in his twenties and he's a bear. You would *not* want to tangle with Bozo.

Between felling and limbing, while his dad twitched out the logs, Bozo carved spruce burls into figurines. One day he proudly showed me an unearthly face he called the "Hide-Behind." He explained, "That's the little critter that haunts the woods but you never see cause it's always sneaking around behind you. It's the lord of the woods."

Watching those trees fall made me dizzy. I paced off one of the tallest timbers.

From butt to crown was about 100 feet. I counted the rings: 80 years' growth.

Two sun hogs stood near the northern boundary shading my neighbor's well. It would be close, but I thought they'd fall clear. Bozo shook his head. It was a good excuse to keep the old heroes around. My neighbor would be pleased. Eventually the woodpeckers would say thanks, too.

We selected the best logs for my pile, and then Ralph hitched the others down to the roadside. On the biggest hitches Ralph drove a team pulling a homemade skipjack. I don't know what a 16-footer 36 inches at the butt weighs, but it took everything those horses had to pull it. A few logs needed cutting into 8-foot lengths or they wouldn't budge.

The trees might not have moved at all if it wasn't for the snow. The weather was with us. The snow lay thick, and we'd started logging right in step with the onset of a stubborn sub-freezing snap. I heard the whole country was frozen clear down to the Florida orange groves. We built some epic bonfires to get through that zero weather.

Logging on snow means easy sliding, no erosion, and the trees come out clean. The only snag is with the horses. They can have a slippery time of it on steep slopes. But if they're shod for snow, it's not bad. The only time a horse went down was from fatigue, not a bad grip.

We shipped out a total of 3800 feet of spruce timber and 12 cords of balsam and spruce pulp. I wound up with 4000 feet of prime sawlogs. We made some money and opened the land for a new generation of trees. It was cold, rough work, but that's all right when you have the Hide Behind on your side.

ONE SAWMILL TO GO

In the hills, timing is everything. April Fools' had come and gone, and the heap of spruce timbers still lay spread across the vegetable garden. Steady rain had been pelting the country for a week. Damn it, I thought, I've gone and backed myself into a corner. I knew that if I didn't get those winter logs off the garden soon I'd be buying the year's food, not growing it. Unfortunately, the driveway was stuck in the middle of mud season. Not oozy enough to prevent cars from getting up the steep grade, but nowhere near ready to support a 14-wheel logging truck. Besides that, the timber didn't add up to half a truckload. It wouldn't be worth hiring a truck, mud or no mud.

But bad timing can be offset by a good neighbor. In this case it was a logger who lives down the valley. He'd just seen the first portable sawmill in town.

"The kerf's just a sixteenth of an inch. You gain 20 percent on your lumber right there!"

Not only did the thin bandsaw blade chew up less lumber than the one-quarter-inch saw at the local mill, but there wasn't any trucking expense. That night I booked the mill, sight unseen.

A week later a gray van scooted up the driveway. Hitched to the back bumper a bright orange two-wheel trailer clattered along. Light rain drizzled down half-heartedly as the van pulled up beside the garden, where I'd been picking parsnips between the timbers. Don Lawrence cut the engine, shouted hello, and jumped down from his seat.

Lawrence appeared to be about 50 and in good shape. He stood well over six feet and wore a maroon Agway cap. On his belt hung a tape measure in a leather pouch and an empty hammer holster. He untied the tarp covering the mill and pulled it aside.

The mill resembled a boat trailer, without the boat. About midpoint on the carriage bed stood an air-cooled, 14-horsepower Kohler engine. The engine was mounted above the trailer on a vertical steel post. A series of rubber belts coupled the engine to the saw blade, or rather, the saw band. It was a shiny steel loop on pulleys, horizontally suspended over the carriage. A set of freshly filed teeth gleamed along the leading edge.

Looking over this lightweight one-man mill, I had a hard time imagining

Lawrence turning my timbers into lumber. When I'd phoned I explained that these were bully trees, including a couple of 7-foot butt logs 30 inches through, and a bunch of 16- and 20-footers, 18 inches at the tapered end.

"Sure your mill can handle this stuff?"

"No problem. You should have seen the pine I cut last week. Got 400 feet out of one log."

Now Lawrence stood frowning at the big timbers. He unsnapped his tape measure and we walked through the garden measuring logs. He took off his cap and scratched his head.

"You have a tractor?" he asked.

"Nope."

"Then we'll have to try it by hand."

What we did first was to unhook the mill from the van. I was surprised how easily it lifted.

"Just weighs 35 pounds at the hitch," he said.

Then Lawrence showed me how to "trig" the wheels so he could turn the mill. He picked up a bean pole and jammed it in front of one tire. Then, while I held the pole wedged in tight, he lifted up the front of the trailer and pivoted the mill to the left. He made a 90-degree turn, and together we pulled the mill halfway across the garden. The mill now stood at the bottom of the slope, below the logs. Lawrence walked back to the van.

"Look at this," he said, pointing inside. The van was lined with dark paneled hardwood cabinets, chests, and stacked drawers, the kind you see in an old New England general store. They were spilling over with nuts, bolts, wrenches, screwdrivers. "Something needs fixing, I don't drive home for a part. I can do it right here."

He took a shovel from the van and dug a hole in front of the uphill trailer wheel. We pulled the mill forward, the wheel dropped into the hole, and the carriage stood laterally level. After adjusting a series of built-in corner jacks, Lawrence finished leveling the mill. Finally, he hooked a pair of steel ramps to the side of the bed and the mill was set for sawing.

Lawrence asked me what kind of lumber I needed. I told him I was planning a barn. I'd sketched in mostly 2 x 6s. But the plan was flexible, which was a good thing, because it turned out that the mill couldn't handle anything longer than 16 feet after all. I decided to make a bunch of the 16-foot spruce into rafters, hung at a 7/12 pitch, which would give me a 24-foot-wide building. Then we could cut the 20-footers into 12s and 8s for studs and loft beams.

I cut down the 20s, and we rolled the first 16-foot log up onto the bed. It was pure grunt work because we had only one peavey. What we lacked in equipment, Lawrence made up in brawn. This mill was classified as a one-man saw, and there's no doubt about it; they meant one *man*. I wielded the bean poles, which made effective levers and skids. Later, hauling in the scattered 16-footers, Lawrence used the winch at the front of the mill. Had I known about

this mobile sawmill back in January, I'd have yarded the logs closer together.

By now the rain had fizzled out and a bright morning sun threw a spotlight on the hills. The knotty old spruce lay prone on the mill bed like an etherized patient waiting for the knife. Lawrence leveled the log with a pink plastic wedge under the taper, then cinched the log tight with a vise action binding clamp. He punched a button, the engine coughed and started. Next to the chugging muffler, the name plate caught my eye: *Wood Mizer.*

I watched Lawrence touch a toggle switch. The sawing unit—engine and saw band together—began to trolley backwards toward the butt of the spruce. When it cleared the end of the stump, he touched another switch. The saw began to descend. He stopped it when the blade dropped just below the butt bark. All this time the Kohler engine had been idling, the steel band still. A small electric motor powered the sawing unit on a track.

Lawrence eyeballed the log. He yanked a lever, the engine roared and the saw began to whirl. Again he set the cutting unit in motion, now forward. The saw screeched into the log. Powdery sawdust sprayed out as the saw sliced sideways down the length of the log. Lawrence stopped the blade and disengaged the engine. He pulled a 16-foot slab off the spruce. Underneath, the fresh cut lumber gleamed white and juicy.

It was my first glimpse of a portable sawmill in action and I understood my neighbor's enthusiasm. This sawmill was doubly mobile. It was a roving mill and the saw itself moved. I'd heard of portable mills before, so cumbersome they needed the equivalent of a logging truck just to get around. And a substantial set-up charge and minimum sawing order. Nothing new there. Those mills required a complex drive system to move the log through the blade. On the other hand, reversing the technique—moving the saw rather than the log—is a real breakthrough.

Of course the ultimate portable mill is the chainsaw lumber maker. Little more than a steel guide plate bolted to the saw, which must be fitted with a special chain, it enables the operator to rip a timber lengthwise. It's handy in remote areas for limited tasks like squaring one or two sides of a log to be used in a cabin. But the chainsaw lumbermaker is slow, tedious and tiring to operate, and inefficient at making decent boards.

Wielding the peavey, Lawrence flipped the log and it lay on its flat surface. He made another cut. Then he sliced off the two remaining slabs. Flip, *buzzzzz* . . . flip, *buzzzzz* . . . . Now the log was roughly square. He squared the log again, this time lopping off four one-inch boards. On the bed now lay a perfect 12- x 14-inch beam, 16 feet long. Lawrence sawed this down the center and then diced each half into seven 2 x 6s. It was the most efficient use of timber I'd ever seen. A conventional sawyer would have squared that log in four quick cuts, discarding the one-inch boards in the slab pile. Not only was the bandsaw's thin blade conserving timber; here was a skilled sawyer making the most of the outside of the log.

We rolled another timber up onto the bed. I noticed that Lawrence's hands were scratched and bleeding.

"Want a pair of gloves?" I asked.

"No thanks. My hands get too hot."

While Lawrence sawed I began to stack and sticker the lumber. It wasn't a flawless sawing operation. The first day he had trouble with some of the bony spruce. The blade had a tendency to ride up and down over the knots, cutting a wavy surface. This was due, in part, to the pitch in the spruce bark. He explained that it would have been smart to saw the lumber in winter, when the bark was frozen, or later when it was bone dry. So we chipped off the bark down the line the saw would follow. This helped prevent the spruce gum from building up on the blade. After the slabs were sliced off, the pitch was no problem. Later, cutting balsam, it wasn't necessary to peel the bark.

The second day Lawrence arrived with a newly sharpened set of saw bands. He'd set the teeth with a slightly wider kerf to get through the tight spruce grain and the knots. Instead of powder, the blade sprayed sawdust with long, thin fibers. The spruce cut perfectly. Lawrence smiled.

"I'm a fussy guy," he said. "I want to cut lumber I'd be proud to use myself."

Later in the day we discovered that loading the logs with the butt end away from the blade made for smoother sawing. It's the same principle as chopping firewood at the small end of the log, which eases splitting.

During the sawing I kept the one-gallon water tank over the blade filled. Lawrence had devised this system to lubricate and cool the saw band. Sawmills sometimes use kerosene for this, but Lawrence preferred water; it's cheap and clean. When he told the people at the Wood Mizer plant about his watering device, they incorporated it into the design.

On the last day, I scaled a handsome spruce log before we rolled it up on the bed. It was a 16-footer, 18 inches at the taper. According to my International Log Rule, it would yield 230 board feet. When we were done toting up the 2 x 6s, 2 x 4s, and boards, I had 290 feet. That's close to a 25 percent increase over the standard sawmill yield.

I was beginning to see my woodlot with a new eye. No more trucking costs. Better than 20 percent increase in timber. Custom cutting, which meant getting exactly the sticks and boards you want from each log. A pile of slabs for firewood and kindling and tomato stakes. Sawdust for animal bedding and blueberry mulch. No shortchanged lumber at the mill. I could even use the slabs to cover the drying lumber.

During lunch Lawrence added to my considerations. He pointed to my firewood log pile.

"There's some good hardwood in there, some of that oak and ash. You might saw it and sticker it up and I'll bet you'd find a cabinet maker who'd buy it."

He went on to tell me about the hardwoods he'd cut for local lumber dealers: butternut, cherry, yellow birch. He said there was even a shingle-maker attachment for the mill.

I thought of all the logs that had rotted here because it didn't pay to truck a small load to the mill; blow-downs, culls cut to clear roads and gardens. In the future, I could use the mobile mill to salvage those logs.

It was over after three days of work. I had 2170 board feet of spruce and balsam, the frame for my new barn, plus a couple of hundred feet of boards. Counting the set-up fee, sawing, and a few hours of jigging ar- und straight labor wage, it averaged out to 15 cents a board foot. That's five cents more than they charge at the local mill. But when you figure the savings in trucking—$100 minimum—and the gain in lumber, plus sawdust and slabs, it's a bargain. No wonder a stream of local woodlot owners ran through here while we were sawing, eager to sign up.

"I used to do mostly carpentry," Don Lawrence told me before he pulled out. "I got this sawmill as a sideline. Now there's no time for anything else."

WATER

BRINGING BACK A SWAMP

There's a spring ritual on my farm that I save for a sunny day in late April when the frost is coming out of the ground. I grab a bucket and a spade and hike off into the woods to a swamp that is peppered with marsh marigolds. I dig up a dozen of them and carry them home to transplant into a mushy stretch of shoreland by my pond.

Marsh marigolds are not an endangered species, but nevertheless I'm pleased to be doing what I can to protect the local population. The jade green plants make for a cheery sight, and I hear the greens are good eating, but I get my fill simply by watching the golden flowers bloom beside the water in May. They glow bright as giant buttercups, heralding spring and something more. The pond is gaining a new dimension. It is becoming a wetland.

That might sound redundant. What could be wetter than a pond? However, a quarter-acre pond eight feet deep is not the same as a marsh. You don't find marsh marigolds in a pond, at least not commonly around the man-made ponds in this territory. A wetland is a swampy plot of earth, the haunt of birds and bugs and snakes. Shallow inland wetlands operate like sponges, holding back floods during a storm, reserving water during a drought, and purifying contaminated water by a natural filtering action. Wetlands provide refuge for all sorts of animals.

They also attract humans. Over the past two centuries, roughly half of the nation's wetlands have been diked, drained, and filled in, and we're still losing about 400,000 acres of wetland every year. Not long ago our local newspaper urged readers to "Guard the Swamps," but that is a formidable task, even in environmentally conscious Vermont, where no laws specifically protect wetlands. Where such laws have been enacted, enforcement is generally lax, due to weak conservation boards and determined developers.

We aren't likely to see the condominiums on Cape Cod melt away into cranberry bogs. But if we can't bring back the original wetlands, why not create new ones? That's where the marsh marigolds come in.

When I decided to turn a wet spot in my meadow into a pond, I found myself faced with a dilemma. In the act of collecting water, I knew I'd be erasing a small piece of wetland. Goodbye woodcock, hello trout. I decided to go ahead and excavate the marsh, promising myself that somehow I'd restore that wetland. Since then I've donated one quarter of the pond's shoreline to wetland preservation.

Naturally, I chose the soggy uphill side of the pond where the spring flows soak the hill. Instead of cross-hatching the bank with curtain drains or covering it with a plank pier, I left it alone. I seeded the ground with a light carpet of grass to prevent erosion, and began to bring in the marsh marigolds. My wife added a spread of day lilies. With the exception of cattails, which I fear would colonize the shallows, we intend to go on transplanting other native wetland flowers and shrubs, and thus invite wetland wildlife to share our pond. For example, alders may attract a family of woodcock or red-winged blackbirds.

I find the appearance of marsh marigolds on the banks of my pond an encouraging sight in the spring. It tells me that TV preachers aren't the only things that can be born again.

TAP YOUR POND FOR FIRE PROTECTION

There's a saying in the hills that the fire department is great at saving cellar holes; and insurance premiums for backwoods homes reflect that pessimistic attitude. The combination of woodstoves, snow-covered roads, and widely scattered volunteer fire fighters make any insurance underwriter edgy. And winter is not the only dangerous season. Last summer, a squad of local firemen raced up to a blazing house, hooked the hose to the tank truck, and found that somebody had forgotten to load the truck with water. Luckily, there was a pond nearby.

A pond may be a rural homeowner's best fire insurance policy. A general-purpose pond as small as one tenth of an acre, nine feet deep at the dam, holds approximately 100,000 gallons. That's more than enough to feed a pump truck all the water necessary to save almost any house or barn, if the truck gets there in time. But to make a homestead even safer, you need an on-site delivery system.

If your pond is sited above your buildings, gravity will deliver the water you need. Indeed, many an old farm was once served by a single gravity-fed that supplied irrigation and livestock water as well as fire protection. Water picks up pressure at roughly half a pound per vertical foot, so a decent fire stream of 70 pounds pressure requires at least 140 feet of "head." Of course, it's possible to make do with less.

If your pond is not situated high enough for a gravity-fed water system, you'll need a pump to take advantage of a pond's fire-fighting potential. There's nothing more pathetic than fighting a blaze with a five-minute chemical extinguisher while a pond ripples nearby, untapped. I once fought a brush fire that way, raking firebreaks, digging trenches, glaring in frustration at the pond 100 yards below. Luckily, late in the afternoon, the wind shifted and the fire died. With a pond-side pump and a hose, I could have doused the fire in minutes and then gone for a swim.

Centrifugal or pressure pumps can deliver more than 100 gallons a minute through 1½-inch hose. Portable models with pull-rope starters—something like a chainsaw engine fitted with plumbing instead of a chain—are ideal for fire fighting. New, one of these two-cycle gasoline pumps costs upwards of $400. Hose runs close to a dollar a foot, and a plastic fire nozzle costs about $15. But before you buy equipment, check with the local fire department; often you'll find second-hand equipment for sale.

The pump should be set up near the pond in a small shelter, ready to go. Make certain there's always a quart of water or antifreeze on hand for priming, and test-start the pump every month. Keep in mind the basic requirements for a home fire pump: it should deliver a fire stream of no less than 100 gallons per minute with pressure at the nozzle of at least 70 pounds.

Next to a pump, a "dry" hydrant is the pond owner's best protection in the event of a fire. A dry hydrant is a freeze-proof tap into the pond. Most of the time it sits empty, connected to the pond by a vertical stem and a pipe that runs below frost level. With the help of a pump (usually aboard a fire truck) the hydrant provides instant access to a reservoir much larger than the truck's own water tank. Usually, a dry hydrant is installed during pond construction; you can add one to an existing pond but it's likely to be expensive. New hydrants are expensive, too, but fire departments, which often replace old ones when they change fittings, sometimes have perfectly good second-hand hydrants for sale.

The main considerations in siting a dry hydrant are to make it accessible to fire trucks and to put it near the house. One of my neighbors has a roadside dry hydrant that's located 50 yards from her pond, close by her home. Another has a similar setup, but it's only 20 feet from pond to hydrant. Naturally, the closer the hydrant to the pond, the less the expense for pipe and installation. Keeping the hydrant plowed out in the winter is crucial, and some highway crews will go out of their way to clear one. It's also smart to put a mesh filter on the inlet pipe to keep silt from clogging it. (Some pond keepers shortcut the dry hydrant completely by allowing a disk of styrofoam to freeze in the ice near shore; the styrofoam can be punched out for quick access to the water. If the pond is any distance from the road, however, this is impractical.)

A pond equipped with a pump or hydrant will provide fire protection, a little peace of mind, and perhaps even more: you may get lower insurance rates, as long as the underwriter is convinced that you will maintain the system properly. One of my neighbors even had his pond dropped from the tax rolls in exchange for a hydrant that would be available to the fire department.

POND POOLING

Hank is a neighbor of mine. He's a truck farmer growing vegetables and grain, and he wants to increase his acreage. That means extra irrigation. A pond would do the trick. Since he lives on a sidehill out beyond the electric line he also wants water power to drive a hydro generator. A pond would put him in the twentieth century. Ten years ago I helped Hank work on pond site selection. But it wasn't until this past August that excavation began. Why the hold up? To build his one-acre reservoir, Hank needed about $6000, and that was way over his head. Then, last year, some friends nearby offered to contribute if they could use the pond for swimming, sauna baths, and skating. Construction is now underway, and Hank is plowing new fields. Coming up: irrigation and hydro power for the farm, and a beach for the neighbors.

Cooperative pond building is appropriate aquaculture. It's not a new idea; people have been digging ponds communally for centuries. But now it involves a new blend of pond makers, community interests, and technique. For instance, an irrigation pond that drops three or four feet in August to quench the crops won't appeal much to swimmers. Or turn an electric turbine. That's why Hank and his partners are excavating in a rich watershed to maximize overflow. Hefty ponds with cascades of surplus water can fulfill more roles than little ones.

There's plenty of room for micro ponds, too. In fact, while the number of our country's farms dwindles in inverse proportion to their acreage, the reverse is true in aquaculture. More ponds are being dug than ever before, and they're getting smaller. The same technology that gives us micro chips and ultralight aircraft enables pond makers to reduce their reservoirs to the size of a washtub. Mostly it's being done with synthetic basin materials and mechanical aeration systems. But pond makers are also taking advantage of traditional small-scale, low-cost Asian and East European aquacultural methods, newly introduced to these shores. Large or small, a pond full of unpolluted water is worth more than a Saudi oil well these days.

Once upon a time the U.S. Department of Agriculture and the Soil Conservation Service helped fund pond makers, but those good old days are fading. Pond-making coops offer a way to take up the slack. And partnerships need not be confined to farming. Ponds often turn up where a landowner teams up with his town. Our local village athletic organization helped gather donations to build a recreation pond. Other pond partnerships involve fishing clubs, land trusts, real estate developments, and fire departments.

One innovative pond blend emerged recently in Wells, Maine. The townspeople were plagued by mosquitoes. Nobody wanted to spray with pesticides. So one family dug a pond and the town put up $1000 to stock it with dragonflies, which are big mosquito guzzlers. Now the mosquitoes get eaten, not the people. And there's a new pond on the planet. The rest of us benefit indirectly from the creation of a wildlife feeding station and wetland. That's pooling your resources.

FROM HAY RAKE TO ROLLING DOCK

For years I've had an itch to build a dock for our pond. Trouble is, I never saw one I liked. At least not until recently, when I got a look at the rolling dock in Donny Prescott's embankment pond on the other side of the mountain. It's the first dock I've seen without those old-fashioned hang-ups: pilings. Instead, the shore-bound end perches on the dam, while the far end stands on a pair of old wagon wheels submerged in a couple of feet of water. The out-bound end juts out just enough so that the drop into the pond basin is overcome by the height of the wheel axle, and the dock stands level. I began ticking off all the points I had against mounting a permanent dock on pilings, and the wheels turned up the solutions.

First off, especially in a small quarter-acre pond like ours, where do you site the dock? Close to a shallow shore might be great for kids and sunbathers and skaters lacing up, but what about trout? The shade cast by a dock can be a life saver for over-heated fish, but it's best in deep water where the trout hang out. The remedy? A dock on wheels that can be rolled around to fit the season and the crop.

Permanently mounting a dock is tricky in ponds where the water level bobs up and down according to runoff and rainfall. A dock over deep water in April may be high and dry come July. On wheels, however, it can be positioned to match the inland tides.

A dock is the perfect place to lash a cage full of fish being fattened for the table. It offers easy access for stocking, feeding and harvest. Cage culture works best with the tie-up out deep, guaranteed against drought. But come winter, after harvest and nearing time for hockey, who wants a dock in center ice? Better to put the dock on wheels, so it can be in deep one day and beached for safe-keeping the next.

Finally, the pond keeper who anticipates touch-up shoreline excavation or dredging would want a dock that could be pulled out of the way during repairs.

Donny told me that he built his rolling dock with a pair of 12-foot, two- by six-inch boards for carrying timbers, one-inch planking, and part of a side delivery hay rake. The old rake was rusting out in the scrap yard alongside Donny's repair shop. After dismantling the rake, he trucked the axle and the wheels to the pond. He mounted the carrying timbers at one end of the axle, nailed down the planks, and clamped the axle in place.

I asked Donny for tips about building my dock.

"I'd try to match the height of the wheels with the slope of the pond basin. The deeper you want to go, the bigger the wheels. Get your axle and wheels first, and remember you can only roll in as deep as the axle. If you want to extend the dock beyond the wheels to go out deeper, you might want to stake down the shore end so it doesn't tip. I think you'll have good luck if you keep a lookout for old farm machinery."

WITCH WAY TO WATER

As clearings go it isn't much, barely a ten-yard square scalping in the woods overshadowed by a ring of spruce and alder. This morning the ground is layered under a vanilla October frost. A pair of blue jays rave away high in the spruce boughs, lit up by the first beams of sun. Down here on the trail to the site, it's cold. Good weather for a chainsaw marathon. No sharp stumps or hanging branches can be allowed to interfere. The clearing must be just right for a backhoe to move in and dig me a well.

The frost is thawing by the time Gary Spooner and Malcolm Ward pull in. Spooner parks the trailer truck. Ward starts up the rubber tire International backhoe. The hoe is school bus yellow and soot smudged, with the headline *Special* across the engine hood. It's chugging hard and the elevated bucket makes it top heavy. Ward stomps on the brakes and the bucket sags to earth. Spooner walks off into the woods. I presume he's going to shake the dew off the lily, but he thrashes around in the underbrush until he emerges with a stick in hand and a satisfied grin. I fill them in with my plans for the well while Ward sits on the backhoe. Spooner stands by whittling the stick with his brass-trimmed pocket knife. Ward has the crewcut edgy look of a Big-Ten quarterback. Spooner's commanding heft and red Musketeer's moustache look right for tackle. I feel like a coach starting a pep talk before the big game.

The plan is to punch a hole in the ground with the backhoe and tap into an aquifer. If it looks good—juicy—we'll build the well. The primary objective is to store water with enough head above the house to produce a natural flow. You really haven't arrived in these hills until you get gravity-fed water. Especially out here beyond the electric line. After nine years of lugging water from a spring, I'm ready. So's Ellen, and she hasn't been around half as long.

I explain that the site is a compromise. I'd rather dig high up on the hill east of the house where greater water pressure would drive a gravity-power shower. But up there are two dry test pits from the past to discourage me. Right now I'd be satisfied with enough to fill the clawfoot tub.

No doubt about it, this place signals water. These alders are big drinkers and the ground bubbles with springs during April and May. I glance down at the melting frost. The land is rocky. I make a silent wish: no ledge, please. There's nothing in the budget for dynamite. When I look up Spooner is striding across the clearing pointing his stick forward. It's a branch worked into the shape of a wishbone, and he holds the two ends at waist level, palms down, with the V aimed ahead.

"Ever see one of these?" Spooner calls as he takes another pass across the clearing. He's crisscrossing over the site with the stick parallel to the earth.

"Sure. It's a dowsing rod. I've got a couple of dry holes up on the hill where the last dowser flunked."

Spooner doesn't reply. His stick dips near the center of the clearing, then lifts. "There's water here, but not much. It feels like a weak vein."

"What about all this ground water? This alder? This place is soaked in the spring."

"Surface runoff," explains Spooner. "You'll be bone dry by summer."

Before I have a chance to absorb the loss of this site and two days work, Spooner is off like a bloodhound heading up the hill east of the house. I'd swear he was being pulled along by that stick. Ward and I trail behind. As Spooner traverses the sidehill, I can see his stick dip and rise. Whenever it dips I recognize a gully that flows in spring. This seems to be a sign that Spooner's wishbone can make dreams of gravity feed come true. Or else he's a clever mimic. After all, test holes get paid for, wet or dry.

Digging for water is risky business. I know people who have drilled artesian wells with great success and considerable expense, and others who never got a drop. One poor guy put all the money he'd saved to build a house into a 600-foot black hole. Besides the risk and expense, a pump is usually required to deliver well water. On the other hand, gravity feed flows free, coming in for as little as three or four hours with a backhoe, a couple of concrete or metal well tiles, and some pipe. A friend just christened a gravity feed system that totaled only $400. He had all the essentials: a source of year-round water not too deep in the ground, at an elevation 15 feet above his kitchen faucet. And good grounds for digging. In the North it's crucial to bury the feed pipe in a trench below frost line—four or five feet deep—or else construct elaborate pipe insulators over ledge and remember to keep the water flowing during the coldest nights. Which can be problematic if your storage isn't sufficient. There's a woman up the valley who must save the flow on sub-zero nights and haul it back up to her shallow well.

When I catch up with Spooner he's pacing back and forth over a patch of hillside shadowed by four sugar maples. Each time he crosses the plot his dowsing stick dives like a magnet to iron. He invites me to try. In my hands the stick is not so responsive. In fact, as I cross the target I'm not sure whether the light tug I feel isn't just wishful thinking. On my second pass Spooner takes hold of my hands and we cross together. The stick swoops down. Now Spooner takes the stick and stands stationary on the spot. The stick screws down steadily, and his face twists into a plum red grimace. He appears to be fighting the pull, like someone losing a tug of war.

Panting, he tells me "I picked up two veins lower down on the hill . . . then I worked up . . . where they come together . . . this is right where they branch apart . . . . The water's down ten feet."

I turn to Ward with a perplexed eye. Is this a circus act? He smiles and shrugs. My head begins to swim. We're overlooking the house 100 yards below. The elevation must be a good 30 or 40 feet. It's a dream site for gravity feed. But the two test pits that failed are half way *down* the hill.

"Hey, I've had people on this hill and nobody dared dig this high. There's no alder. No springs."

Spooner points up at the maples towering over us. He tells me that each of those trees needs 40 gallons of water a day, in summer, when the water's low.

"I'm not worried about water," he says. "What I'm worried about is ledge." He tosses the stick aside. "Some people have the gift. But I don't know anybody who can tell you if there's ledge."

The sun glows in the south. The leaves have fallen, all but the fiery shreds on the maples above us. This seems to augur well. Spooner's confidence is getting contagious. Still, it's going to be a mess getting the backhoe up the hill. The ground is strewn with brush, logs, pulpwood bolts, and stovewood—remnants of the logging operation that stalled while I cleared the well site. Wouldn't it work out best to postpone the digging for a couple of days and open up a road and a new clearing? Nope. They'd rather take a chance crashing through the slash. The sun feels warm today, but the clock's ticking toward the big freeze. If there's going to be running water for us this winter it's got to happen now. These guys are booked solid.

"Everybody puts off digging 'til the last second," Ward scolds. "Then they all call up when the frost hits." He shakes his head. I brace myself. This is it. You either go with the flow or forget it. That's the way it happens in the hills.

Ward assaults the slope backwards, bucket forward to balance against the steep grade, uphill tires rearing off the ground. He rides in the manner of a jockey at a gallop, way up out of the saddle, but instead of stirrups he's standing on the brakes. He looks ready to leap. He is. Last week on a steep hill he rolled the Special and had to jump.

It's a surreal steeplechase with Ward riding the hoe over the logs and brush. When he encounters anything massive enough to stall the climb, he replies with brute force. He swings his hydraulic bucket back and forth and clobbers obstacles out of the path. This might be a job for Superman but Ward handles the hoe like Godzilla.

A spruce stands on the downhill edge of the site where Ward needs to set up. I offer to fetch the chainsaw, but he declines. Bucket high, he pushes against the trunk. It bends. It bows low like a mighty tree in a gale. Roots burst from the ground fierce as angry snakes. The spruce drops. Ward smiles. The digging begins.

I've grown to savor the sight of a backhoe at work. It makes my back say thanks. Spooner seems pleased, too. He pulls a pipe out of his Hopalong Cassidy shirt pocket and lights up. Eddies of rum-soaked tobacco smoke swirl around us and blend with diesel exhaust. This sweet and sour blend mingles with the sharp scent of fresh cut earth and grows into another blend, which is in turn laced with bursts of smoke from flinty stones struck by the bucket. At the edge of the dig I breathe in the brimstone flavor of the shaft.

The hole is now about three feet deep and a bucket wide. Spooner leans over it, between scoops, attentive as a chef checking his soup. He shouts something through the hoe's thunder.

"Smell the water?"

Smell water?

The hole deepens. Ward dumps the earth downhill to prevent the pit from slumping in. Beneath the dark forest topsoil the soil yellows, a distressing sight.

"Sand," I tell him.

"Better than ledge."

The hoe digs. The heap of earth grows. Spooner draws on his pipe. A cloud of smoke floats across the hole. He declares he can *feel* water. It's true. A mist from the shaft chills my face. It's close to the feeling you get walking on a freshly plowed garden. Moist. But this is meant to be a well, not a garden.

The hoe hits rock. We all give the rock a close inspection. Is it the dreaded ledge? Ward grins. The hoe attacks. Steel talons rip at the earth. Puffs of flinty smoke swirl up from the hole. A black boulder pops out tight in the grip of the bucket. Big smiles. We haven't moved a step.

I try to imagine ancestors who dug for water with sticks. They were lucky if they had a shovel. Real lucky, a bucket hooked to a gin pole with block and tackle. Not many decades ago two good men needed a week to dig a 10-foot well. And there might not be a drop at the bottom.

Measured by steel tape the shaft is six feet deep. It looks like a grave. The soil coming out feels sandy.

Nine feet. Still sandy. The hoe pauses. Ward is not smiling.

"The stick said ten feet," Spooner reminds us.

"I can't go any deeper," says Ward.

I begin to think I can't either. I imagine this quest will strike my neighbors as deeply far-fetched.

What's that hole there? Wishing well?

Spooner waves his pipe. The backhoe arm rises from the shaft. Polished by the earth, the bucket shines like silver. Spooner steps into the bucket and then invites me. Gently we're lowered down into the hole.

It's cool at the bottom. Underfoot, the soil is sticky. Spooner compresses a clump of dirt in his fist. When he opens his hand, we see a ball of soil holding together. Clay. Clay holds water. He pitches the ball up and Ward catches.

"I'm going to try another spot," Ward hollers.

"Wait up!"

"Don't worry," Spooner says, "he's just moving the bucket."

We ride up. The hoe pulls back. A few feet lower down the hill it paws at the ground. Soon the landing beside the shaft has been lowered. From the new site the digging resumes.

Now we've tapped a solid layer of deep blue clay, rich and dark and moist. No telling how wide the layer spreads out. It pans underneath the shaft all around. It occurs to me that this is almost as good as finding chocolate at the bottom of a cheesecake. Even the clay dumped on the sandpile looks like icing. These thoughts arise because it's way past noon and we've skipped lunch. It's a rare experience. Usually I work with carpenters. Carpenters know exactly what they're doing. They have plans. Solid citizens. Three squares a day. But well diggers are gamblers. There's too much acid in the stomach for lunch.

We're down to ten feet. I pray for a geyser to burst out, but there's only that blue layer of clay. Spooner waves for the bucket. We drop down. A band of clay two feet thick encircles the base of the shaft. Is that a drop of water? Nope, a pebble. Spooner crouches at the base of the shaft. The walls of the shaft have been glazed smooth and sealed by the bucket. Spooner scratches at the clay. His fingernails dig into the glaze. Suddenly, like evening stars appearing one by one, tiny fountains of water sparkle around us. Water begins to pour from the scratches in the clay. We shout it up together: *water!*

I slap Spooner on the back and shake his hand. The ground is bubbling under our boots. Spooner waves his pipe.

"Let's get out of here."

We step into the bucket, there's a bone-shaking backfire, and quick as a champagne cork we're out.

One story ends, another begins. It's been a couple of weeks' ditching and plumbing since that day on the hill. On the table beside me sits a Mason jar full of well water, fresh as dew. There's also a bill: tiles, PVC pipe, crushed stone, equipment time, labor. It all checks out except for one missing item. I call up Spooner.

"You forgot the dowsing," I tell him.

"Nope," he says, "I never charge for dowsing. It's a gift."

EPILOGUE

Unlike a house, which is never really finished, a book must come to an end. But when? For me, it's like the feeling you get at the end of a long day in the woods. The time has come to head home. If you stay out too long you're bound to mess up.